Elsa Schiaparelli

CREATIVE HOMES

INSIDE THE PRIVATE WORLDS OF AUSTRALIA'S STYLE MAKERS

HarperCollins*Publishers*

HarperCollins*Publishers*

First published in Australia in 2005
by HarperCollinsPublishers Pty Limited
ABN 36 009 913 517
A member of the HarperCollinsPublishers (Australia) Pty Limited Group
www.harpercollins.com.au

HarperCollins*Publishers*
25 Ryde Road, Pymble, Sydney, NSW 2073, Australia
31 View Road, Glenfield, Auckland 10, New Zealand
77–85 Fulham Palace Road, London, W6 8JB, United Kingdom
2 Bloor Street East, 20th floor, Toronto, Ontario M4W 1A8, Canada
10 East 53rd Street, New York NY 10022, USA

ISBN 0 7322 8261 6

Cover and text design by Tracy Lines and Natalie Winter
Front cover image photograph by Lucas Allen; styled by Glen Proebstel (home of Zahava Elenberg)
Back cover image photograph by Anson Smart (home of Jane Roarty)
Author photograph by Prue Ruscoe
Typeset in DIN Regular 8/12.5

Produced in Hong Kong on 157gsm Chinese Matt Art

5 4 3 2 1   05 06 07 08

CREDITS: Lee Mathews's chair (page 2): stylist Megan Morton; photos Con Poulos. **Lyn Gardener's** bathroom (page 5): stylist Christine Rudolph; photos Mikkel Vang. **Adrian Lewis's** living room (page 6): photos Chris Chen. **Stephen Ormandy & Louise Olsen** (page 10): stylist Megan Morton; words Prue Rushton; photos Prue Ruscoe. **Tetsuya Wakuda** (page 16): stylist Megan Morton; words Cyndi Tebbel; photos Louise Lister. **Adrian Lewis** (page 20): words Nicole Lehmann; photos Chris Chen. **Peter Crisp** (page 26): stylist Megan Morton; words Cyndi Tebbel; photos Anson Smart. **Belinda Seper** (page 32): stylist Megan Morton; words Marion Von Adlerstein; photos Prue Ruscoe. **Dare Jennings** (page 36): stylist Megan Morton; words Prue Rushton; photos David Matheson. **Marcia Hosking** (page 40): words Jenna Reed Burns; photos Chris Chen. **Jackie O** (page 46): stylist Megan Morton; words Carl Hammerschmidt; photos Anson Smart. **Jane de Teliga** (page 50): words Marion Von Adlerstein; photos Prue Ruscoe. **Julie Paterson** (page 54): stylist Marcus Hay; words Prue Rushton; photos Elsa Hutton. **Neil Perry** (page 58): stylist Megan Morton; words Cyndi Tebbel; photos Jonny Valiant. **Leona Edmiston** (page 62): stylist Megan Morton; words Eliza O'Hare; photos Con Poulos. **Akira Isogawa** (page 68): stylist Megan Morton; words Marion Von Adlerstein; photos Anson Smart. **Jane Roarty** (page 72): words Cyndi Tebbel; photos Anson Smart. **Eva Hannah** (page 78): stylist Glen Proebstel; words Carrie Hutchinson; photos Con Poulos. **Zahava Elenberg** (page 82): stylist Glen Proebstel; words Isobel King; photos Lucas Allen. **Gabrielle Courtenay** (page 88): stylist Margot Braddon; words Jenna Reed Burns; photos Prue Ruscoe. **Lyn Gardener** (page 92): stylist Christine Rudolph; words Rachelle Unreich; photos Mikkel Vang. **Amanda Briskin** (page 96): stylist Megan Morton; words Rachelle Unreich; photos Lucas Allen. **Simmone Logue** (page 100): stylist Megan Morton; words Nikki Goldstein; photos Michael Wee. **Donald Campbell**, beach house (page104): stylist Megan Morton; words Marion Von Adlerstein; photos Anson Smart. City house (page 106): stylist Vanessa Holden; words Nicole Lehmann; photos Gerard Needham. **Lee Mathews** (page 112): stylist Megan Morton; words Prue Rushton; photos Con Poulos. **Stephen Jolson** (page 118): stylist Megan Morton; words Stephen Crafti; photos Lucas Allen. **Jacqueline Coates** (page 122): stylist Megan Morton; words Carrie Kableau; photos Chris Chen. **Deborah Hutton** (page 126): stylist Megan Morton; words Cyndi Tebbel; photos Anson Smart. **Giovanni D'Ercole** (page 130): stylist Justine Osborne; words Christina Larmer; photos Richard Powers. **Lisa Wilkinson & Peter FitzSimons** (page 134): stylist Megan Morton; words Cyndi Tebbel; photos Prue Ruscoe; portrait of Lisa and Peter by Amanda Prior. **David Bromley & Tori Dixon-Whittle** (page 138): words Jenna Reed Burns; photos Prue Ruscoe. **Pam Easton** (page 144): stylist Megan Morton; words Prue Rushton; photos Prue Ruscoe. **Lydia Pearson** (page 148): stylist Megan Morton; words Prue Rushton; photos Prue Ruscoe. **Charlie Brown** (page 152): stylist Megan Morton; words Nikki Goldstein; photos Chris Chen. **David Adams** (page 156): stylist & words Deborah Bibby; photos Michael Wee. **Carole Muller** (page 160): words Jenna Reed Burns; photos Chris Chen. **Saskia Havekes** (page 164): stylist Tami Christiansen; words Carrie Kablean; photos Nathalie Krag. **Natalie Bloom** (page 170): stylist Megan Morton; words Eliza O'Hare; photos Prue Ruscoe. **Ken Done** (page 174): stylist Megan Morton; words Carrie Kablean; photos Michael Wee. **Megan Morton** (page 178): stylist Megan Morton; words Alexander Kendrew; photos Con Poulos. **Iain Halliday** (page 182): stylist Megan Morton; words Cyndi Tebbel; photos Richard Bailey. **Archie and Henry** (page 191): stylist Megan Morton; photos Con Poulos.

A big thank you to all the immensely talented photographers, stylists and writers whose work is featured in this book. In particular I must thank Megan Morton, who has undertaken the lion's share of the production/styling with great good humour and skill. And my thanks, too, to Tracy Lines, creative director of *Inside Out,* who was instrumental in shaping the design of this book. Justine Knapp's organisation skills were of great help.

bathe

CONTENTS

INTRODUCTION

It is very easy to become seduced by other people's homes and I willingly acknowledge that I am particularly susceptible in this regard. Show me a minimalist apartment with killer views and spare designer furnishings, and I am mentally de-cluttering my own home. On the other hand, a trip to a charming dilapidated seaside cottage makes me consider relocating before you can say *objet trouvé*. Many of the homes in this book evoke the same sensation because they are so well considered, and so well executed, that whatever style of interiors their owners have chosen to adopt they convey it with complete aplomb.

It was after some discussion that we settled on the title *Creative Homes* for this, the first book from the archives of *Inside Out* magazine. It seemed to fit with the ethos of the magazine that style is not about dollars – it is about a sensibility, an attitude and an expression of personality.

We qualified the title – with 'inside the private worlds of Australia's style makers' – because these people, whether they acknowledge it or not, have shaped the contemporary Australian aesthetic, be it in the realm of homewares, food, fashion, art or interior design. Listening to how they articulate their feelings, I was surprised by the levels of connection with their homes and the pleasure that comes from creating a space that expresses how they want to live. As Lydia Pearson, of fashion design duo Easton Pearson, says, 'I didn't want something that looked ethnic or European. I wanted a pastiche of different feelings and styles.'

The people featured in this book manage to balance creativity and informality, passion without the pretension. There is also a sort of 'devil may care' attitude that marks the truly creative spirit. Julie Paterson, of textile company Cloth, has left patches of plaster and paint exposed on her walls so that the patina of time and history is still visible; Lydia Pearson's lounge room ceiling is painted in bold stripes of red and white; while artist David Bromley has painted a mural directly onto the wall behind his bed. All three denote exuberant decorative statements and have the effect of making me, for one, feel timid and conventional in my attitude to my own home.

There is also the ability to see beauty where others fail to perceive it. A disused boarding house, a rundown cottage, a '60s warehouse or an apartment filled with partition walls and shag-pile carpet were the dubious starting points for some. Others have transformed something seemingly ordinary into a place where their collections, their use of colour and their unerring eye for what works, have created an intensely personal environment. As boutique owner Belinda Seper says, 'There is immense beauty in imperfection, and I think my house reflects that.'

The success of these interiors comes, in part, from time and thoughtfulness. Time spent collecting and curating furniture, objects and artworks; thought as to their placement, their relationship to the colours and objects around them, as part of an overall scheme. As Jane Roarty, executive fashion editor at *marie claire*, points out, 'It is about gradually collecting and adding personality, so that it keeps evolving.' There is no way these looks can be achieved at a one-stop shop. It is the very opposite of the 'decorate in a weekend' culture we see all around us.

It is interesting that style-wise there is a complete independence of thought. While some homes might give a nod to Europe or Asia, there is no one look – diversity does prevail. There are, however, recurring passions. There is a love of objects with a history, which manifests itself in many forms. In the case of Melbourne jeweller Adrian Lewis, it is a penchant for antiques, heirlooms and market finds which he admits engenders the 'experience of calmness'. At the other extreme there is artist David Bromley, who is enthused by Depression-era furniture for its make-do inventiveness, and in the same aesthetic camp, Julie Paterson celebrates rag rugs for their essentially unglamorous but still charming qualities.

Stephen Ormandy and Louise Olsen of Dinosaur Designs are collectors of mid-century furniture which they mix with a melting pot of finds from their travels, and their own jewel-like collections of resin vases, plates and cups. Collecting art is a passion for Stephen and Louise, and, they point out, it is driven by aesthetics, not investment. In their egalitarian interior, $10 prints hang alongside works of higher value.

Travel is an ongoing source of inspiration that shapes everything for some and significant elements for others. Dave Adams, a serious traveller for work and pleasure, has fashioned a new house in Sydney's Palm Beach entirely in adobe for its tactile quality. He has used Mughal Indian screens as structural devices and Moroccan chandeliers and rugs from Kabul as decoration. His is a truly cultural cocktail which still manages to work.

In a much slicker context, architect Stephen Jolson has decorated his home with vibrant, large-scale photographs taken on his travels in North Africa and India. They animate an otherwise clean, modern space and provide a context for the clever mixing of an original Le Corbusier chaise with coffee tables fashioned from Cambodian rain drums. And yes, it does hang together.

This book represents a range of homes across the cost spectrum. In some it is a combination of money and taste, while others are the result of an inbuilt sensibility and artful approach to what they own and how they display it. Artist Gabrielle Courtenay talks about achieving a 'silk look on a polyester budget' and, with her intuitive colour sense, she has done just that.

Looking through the houses here, I was heartened by the life-affirming philosophies of these 40 people. Their attitude, albeit to material things, doesn't feel like a hollow exercise of style over substance, but rather the substance itself – a genuine emotional connection with their home and the objects with which they surround themselves. I found their stories, their ideas and their approach to life incredibly inspiring and I genuinely hope that exploring their homes in this book gives you the same experience.

Karen McCartney

STEPHEN ORMANDY AND LOUISE OLSEN DESIGNERS

'WE WANTED TO BE BY THE SEA – EVEN JUST A HINT OF BLUE SOMEWHERE WOULD DO,' SAYS LOUISE OLSEN, WHO SHARES HER HOME OVERLOOKING THE OCEAN WITH HUSBAND STEPHEN ORMANDY AND DAUGHTER CAMILLE. WITH LIANE ROSSLER, STEPHEN AND LOUISE MAKE UP THE TRILOGY THAT IS DINOSAUR DESIGNS. YOU CAN SEE EVIDENCE OF THIS EVERYWHERE YOU LOOK IN THEIR CONVERTED FEDERATION HOME IN SYDNEY'S BRONTE. A STRIKING KALEIDOSCOPE OF THEIR COLOURED GLASS VASES, RESIN BOWLS, DINNER PLATES AND CERAMIC DISHES INHABITS ALMOST EVERY

Far left, offbeat shapes from Dinosaur Designs arranged along a shelf in Stephen Ormandy and Louise Olsen's home; **centre**, Louise, Stephen and daughter Camille; **this page**, one of many collections which get moved around, includes Dinosaur Designs resin vases, a Balinese coral sculpture, and a sand-blasted Murano glass sculpture.

Right, on a kitchen windowsill Dinosaur Designs vases sit beside other glass finds; **below**, Stephen made the wire sculpture which holds some of Louise's jewellery; **opposite page**, the living room features a typical mix of beloved artworks and objects. The rattan chair and footstool were brought back from a trip to Southeast Asia.

surface. This says a lot about why they started their homewares business in the first place. 'We'd come through art school and lived in the share house where no-one really cared,' says Stephen. 'But when we started decorating our own homes, we wanted nice things.'

To Stephen and Louise, home has always had the same meaning: it is 'Somewhere that we love being, surrounded by the things that we love,' says Stephen. As their business expands to overseas, they've also started applying adjectives like 'peaceful' and 'relaxing' to their list of needs. 'During the week, we have a lot of people working around us,' says Louise, 'So it's nice to come back here and recharge.'

Every surface of the house is an excuse to display the things the couple have collected over the years, either locally or while travelling. Mostly, they are things found together. If not, it's rare that they would disagree – they've understood each other's eye and taste since they met at art school 20 years ago. The displays tend to move around from bookcases to walls, to shelves above the kitchen sink to table tops.

Most of the images or sculptures decorating their home have been carefully sought out at auctions and gallery openings. There are artworks in every room of the house – even the kitchen – and many have been given to them by family. Others are by artist friends who swap their works for Dinosaur Designs pieces. Nevertheless, Stephen and Louise are adamant they never buy for investment purposes, and they're not precious about mixing originals with a $10 print they found at a market.

'It's just about following your eye and what moves you,' says Louise. And they couldn't bear to part with any of their pieces.

PAUSE
PRIVATE VIEW
GLENN MURCUTT
Japan
Adornment
ANDREA PALLADIO
MAX BECKMANN
PETER ROBB
Goodbye Picasso
FRANCISCO GOYA
GAUGUIN
marc newson
HENRI MATISSE

This page, when the dining table isn't being used it becomes a place to display the couple's own work and objects picked up during trips to Fiji and Bali; **opposite page**, the black and white mural in the kitchen is by Dorothy Napangardi.

Tetsuya's 'home away from home' above his city restaurant. **Left**, the tea set was a gift from a friend in Japan; the painting is *Crossing the Line* by Brad Monro; **below**, the master chef; **opposite page**, Tetsuya's cookbook collection is displayed behind a black leather sofa. The red sculpture is *Tarantella* by Russell McQuilty.

TETSUYA WAKUDA RESTAURATEUR

ABOVE TETSUYA'S WORLD-RENOWNED RESTAURANT IN THE CENTRE OF SYDNEY'S CBD IS HIS 'HOME AWAY FROM HOME': A LARGE PRIVATE OFFICE, COMPLETE WITH KITCHEN, COMFY LEATHER SOFAS, FAVOURITE PIECES OF ART AND A BOOKCASE HOLDING HALF OF HIS EXTENSIVE COOKBOOK COLLECTION. IT'S WHERE HE TEACHES AND DELEGATES TO STAFF, CHECKS ON PRODUCE AND MAKES UP THE RECIPES WHICH HAVE MADE HIS DEGUSTATAION MENU JUSTIFIABLY FAMOUS. A NIGHT OWL WHO GETS BY ON LITTLE SLEEP, TETSUYA, OR 'TETS' TO HIS FRIENDS, WILL OFTEN END HIS

ART TODAY
FOOD & FRIENDS
GREAT DESSERTS
CONRAN
Nigel Slater Appetite
ALASTAIR LITTLE
NIGELLA LAWSON
rick stein's seafood

The city apartment. **Right**, among Tetsuya's striking artworks is Grace Burzese's *Writing White (Vertical)*; **below**, in the bedroom the vibrancy of Grace Burzese's *Double Speak* contrasts with the calm decor; **opposite page**, Tetsuya on his sleep-inducing lounge. Behind him is *Scape* by Mark Draper.

working day late then walk the short distance to his real apartment, in a city tower block. This apartment is where he recharges. It is up high, so he can gaze out at the beauty of the city, and enclosed within it Tetsuya finds the peace and solitude he needs away from work.

Tetsuya's luxurious living rooms are furnished with Italian pieces that provide the ultimate in comfort – essential for someone who spends most of his time on his feet.

His love of art is highlighted by paintings large enough to fill the walls. In the living room at home is *Scape* by Mark Draper and he also owns several Brad Monro pieces. Other pieces of fine art from Japan, his birthplace, such as hand-carved wooden sake bowls, blend in with the overall cosmopolitan feel.

After a week of the high life, and the hustle and bustle of a busy restaurant, Tetsuya usually feels like a little grounding. On Friday nights he escapes to his boat at Jones Bay in Pyrmont. 'I have a little boat, an eight-metre Beneteau. It's not a yacht; I don't have the patience. It's a cruiser: turn it on, push the button, engine moves and you're off. I don't drive a car, but I love driving boats,' he explains. 'It's the freedom. Some people like flying, but this is much safer.'

On the weekends he can be found watching fishing programs on The Lifestyle Channel in Observatory Tower. But he says, his couch at home is so comfortable, he often falls asleep before he's watched too much.

Tetsuya's apartments, like his restaurant, speak of a masculine but sophisticated aesthetic where calm and an enjoyment of beauty prevail.

BOUCHON

ADRIAN LEWIS JEWELLER

LIKE HIS JEWELLERY DESIGNS, ADRIAN LEWIS'S APARTMENT REFLECTS HIS PASSION FOR ANTIQUES AND HISTORY. 'I REALLY DO BELIEVE IN THE POWER OF YOUR OWN PLACE AND BEING SURROUNDED BY THE THINGS THAT YOU LOVE,' HE SAYS. HIS ONE-BEDROOM GROUND-FLOOR APARTMENT IS TUCKED AWAY IN A CUL-DE-SAC IN THE PRESTIGIOUS MELBOURNE SUBURB OF TOORAK. WELL-KNOWN ARCHITECT SIR ROY GROUNDS DESIGNED THE AWARD-WINNING APARTMENT BLOCK IN 1940, USING PRACTICAL AND INEXPENSIVE MATERIALS FROM THE WAR YEARS,

Far left, one of Adrian Lewis's jewellery designs, a fleur-de-lys with a black pearl; **centre**, Adrian in his Toorak flat; **this page**, the living room. The velvet stool was made by a friend, the wire lamp base is by Adrian.

ADRIAN LEWIS

Right, the living room features a mix of styles. Masks from Ghana sit on top of a 1940s Swedish cabinet bought locally; the 1950s low chair came from Camberwell markets. The Italian glass table is a 1960s find with a base made from gilded metallic sheaves of wheat.

such as concrete, which achieved a far from cheap-looking result. Adrian admires Grounds's ability to bring out the beauty in these materials and his way of paring back.

'When designing this block of apartments, Roy Grounds considered light levels and simplicity of form,' says Adrian. 'There are few fancy details such as skirting boards and cornices, so the building hasn't dated. The fireplace has no mantelpiece, for example – it's just a hole in the wall. My apartment doesn't belong to any particular period and I love that.'

His style has matured over the years, although a stack of artworks, a garage full of treasures, family heirlooms and marketplace whims satisfy inevitable creative impulses. 'I like clean lines and I have an obsession with white,' says Adrian. 'I like some contemporary pieces, but I think the whole *Wallpaper** magazine look has become a bit sad. Pieces by top designers such as Charles and Ray Eames have been commercialised. They're beautiful designs, but now you see them everywhere, in every hotel lobby. I want to stay away from that in my interior. I want something more individual.'

Adrian has grown up surrounded by magnificent examples of design from many different periods. His mother, a one-time dealer of antiques and a compulsive hoarder of pieces of great pedigree, has instilled in him an eye for the exquisite. But he insists his personal style varies greatly from his mother's. His mother uses colour lavishly. His own love of white may, in fact, be a backlash against growing up with a blood-red bedroom. 'I came from such a coloured world,' he jokes. 'It was enough to put me off colour for the rest of my life!'

This page, Adrian's books and magazines are stacked in piles under a table made by a friend; **opposite page**, a tribal chair bought from a dealer in African artefacts sits beside a mirrored display cabinet now used as a bedside table. The gilt altarpiece came from Spain.

PETER CRISP GLASS ARTIST

A SHEEP FARM IN NEW SOUTH WALES ISN'T WHERE YOU'D EXPECT TO FIND ONE OF THE WORLD'S BEST GLASS ARTISTS. YET GAP RANGE, AN 810 HECTARE PROPERTY SOUTH OF YASS ON THE HUME HIGHWAY, IS WHERE PETER CRISP FINDS THE INSPIRATION TO CREATE HIS EXQUISITE COLLECTIONS AND ONE-OFF PIECES OF ART GLASS AND TABLEWARE. THERE HAVE BEEN CRISPS IN THE DISTRICT SINCE THE 1930s, AND PETER, HIS MOTHER HELEN AND HORTICULTURALIST BROTHER SANDY ARE KEPT BUSY RUNNING THE MANY CREATIVE ENTERPRISES THEY HAVE DEVELOPED. APART FROM THE 7000

Far left, a cairn-based fountain is one of the sculptural elements dotted around Peter Crisp's property; **centre**, Peter relaxing outside his 1940s cottage; **this page**, the trompe l'oeil effect around the door of Peter's former study was painted by Peter and a friend, Peta Seaton. The Belgian floor rug has been in the family since the 1930s.

PETER CRISP

Right, the kitchen. Above the fireplace is a landscape by Annabel Butler, the table was custom made; **below**, one of Peter's tableware designs, Ottoman, is a best seller in the US; **opposite page**, the bedroom features a 1920s chandelier found in a junk shop. On the wall behind the bed is *Chartreuse* by Zimbabwean artist Michelle Purves.

resident sheep, the property houses galleries, including one that showcases a number of Peter's creations, and The Performance Space, a venue for concerts and exhibitions of other artists' work.

Peter's small country cottage, built in the mid-1940s, is where he retreats when he's not working in his studio or talking to admirers. Out the front a frayed armchair invites quiet reflection and a place to watch the world go by. Inside, Peter's natural artistic style is everywhere, in the decorative tones, the fine art and vintage furniture. A trompe l'oeil around the wooden French doors leading into the living room was inspired by frescoes from Pompeii, and the room is filled with family heirlooms, including an organ that belonged to his grandmother and a Belgian rug that has been in the family since the 1930s.

The warmth and modest style of Peter's cottage reflects the understated nature of this quiet achiever. Over the past 20 years, his work has become highly collectable, with pieces held in galleries and private collections all around the world. He's a big name in high-end department stores like Barneys in New York and Asprey in London, while his tableware graces the homes of celebrities such as Tina Turner and the dining room of Britain's Waterside Inn, where three-star Michelin chef Michel Roux puts Peter's service through the dishwasher three times a day.

'I'm a much happier individual getting back to the one-offs and mixing that with the tableware and design work,' says the artist. 'I really need to concentrate on my work, but sometimes I enjoy the weeding and I'm happy to be in the garden,' he says. 'I rarely work on weekends these days, but if I do I prefer to isolate myself in The Performance Space or in my cottage.'

This page, Peter's god-daughter, Josephine, dancing in The Performance Space shed on the property. The shed, which has timber floors and corrugated iron walls, has been used for hosting concerts and the occasional ball; **opposite page**, in summer, guests are often wined and dined under a canopy of New Zealand hybrid willows. Up to 200 people can be seated at a long table.

BELINDA SEPER BOUTIQUE OWNER

'IT'S BASICALLY A BIG SPACE THAT I MANAGE TO PUT ALL MY BITS AND PIECES IN,' IS HOW FASHION ICON BELINDA SEPER VIEWS HER SYDNEY HOME IN INNER-CITY PADDINGTON. SINCE HER LIFE IS WORK-CENTRED, BELINDA DOES THE NEXT BEST THING TO LIVING 'ABOVE THE SHOP': SHE LIVES A FIVE-MINUTE WALK FROM HER STORES. THE WEATHERBOARD WORKER'S COTTAGE SHE SHARES WITH HER DAUGHTER SOPHIE (WHEN THE LATTER IS NOT AT BOARDING SCHOOL IN THE COUNTRY) IS THE IDEAL SPACE FOR AN INSATIABLE COLLECTOR. 'I'M NOT MUCH OF A RENOVATOR,' SHE ADMITS,

Far left, a print of a magnolia, Belinda Seper's favourite flower, sits on her desk; **centre**, Belinda wrapped in a scarf from her collection; **this page**, the driftwood chair was found at a craft shop near Byron Bay. Belinda found *Edith*, a 1932 oil painting, in a flea market in Brussels.

Right, the living room's Oriental corner features an antique Chinese firescreen and a table with mother-of-pearl inlay; **below**, a mix of colour and styles make an effective display in a bookshelf; **opposite page**, in keeping with Belinda's love of imperfection, mismatched chairs are grouped around a dining table.

adding that she's content to 'splash a bit of paint around. There's an immense beauty in imperfection and I think my house reflects that. I'm just passionate about trawling endless flea markets, antique markets and junk shops, then surrounding myself with things I love.'

No matter where she goes on numerous yearly buying trips, Belinda delights in the thrill of finding trophies to bring home. Every piece in her house has a story: the painting bought for £25 in London's Portobello Road; the portrait (on the 1930s French table) from Porte de Vanves flea market in Paris; the chair found at 'an old market barn somewhere in the Southern Highlands'; the 1940s cut-glass lamp from a market in Milan; the big piece of driftwood from Indonesia. 'I love "resting places" in the home,' she says, 'little collections of things. Sometimes, during the day, I'll just glance at them and I get a lift. I think, yes, everything's going to be fine.'

Her frequent trips to the country to visit Sophie is always an opportunity for a good old browse through junk shops. She marvels at what she finds: 'This is where one person's trash can become another's treasure, where you find things for $10, $20 or $30. I'm not looking for anything in particular, but I know it if I see it.'

Any time off from her mobile life is spent at home. Her garden is small, but she does 'poke around there at weekends. It's important to be connected to nature in some way,' she explains.

As for the house itself, Belinda is not in the least precious. 'My home is important to me, but it's not everything,' she says. 'The rest of my life is so rewarding that I don't place any more emphasis on my home than my stores.'

DARE JENNINGS FOUNDER OF MAMBO

A TOUCH OF THE ASIAN JUNGLE IS HARDLY WHAT YOU'D EXPECT IN THE MIDST OF SYDNEY'S COASTAL SUBURB OF TAMARAMA BEACH, YET IT'S WHAT ATTRACTED DARE JENNINGS, FOUNDER OF MAMBO, TO HIS CLIFF-TOP HOME. THE GARDEN OF BIG, GREEN-LEAFED PALMS AND TREES, AND RUNNING WATER AND PONDS GREETS YOU AT THE ENTRANCE TO THE THREE-STOREY PROPERTY HE SHARES WITH HIS WIFE, MALIWAN, AND THEIR SON HARRY. 'THE THING I LIKED ABOUT THE HOUSE WAS THAT IT'S SHIELDED BY THE GARDEN AND A WALL. IN ASIA, I WAS IMPRESSED

Far left, the top floor of Dare Jennings's tropical house looks out over the ocean; **centre**, Dare at home; **this page**, the living area contains works by the artists who helped make Mambo famous – and a collection of Dare's musical toys, including a Rickenbacker guitar once owned by the guitarist from Midnight Oil.

Right, urn-like scupltures by Gerry Wedd and a 'Madonna' surfboard by David McKay in a corner of the dining area; **below**, the kitchen is used constantly by both Dare and Maliwan; **opposite page**, the bathroom occupies one of the best spots in the house. The shower has an ocean view.

that you can be in a grubby area and knock on a door and it opens into this beautiful garden.'

Inside the living room, a profusion of stuffed toys and child-proofing equipment amidst an impressive amount of chrome and sound equipment shows how a blokey bachelor pad has been adapted for family living. 'It's funny, because I went from having a house I could show off to having a home – and it's a million times more satisfying,' he says. Throughout all of these changes, the sea has been an important part of his lifestyle: 'On warm days I can pull back the doors and smell the ocean.'

Hanging on or leaning against a wall of the living room are prints and artworks by people who've helped create the Mambo look, names such as Martin Sharp, Paul Worstead and Garry Shead. In this space there's also David McKay's 'Madonna' surfboard, and a number of urn-like sculptures by Gerry Wedd.

Fortunately Dare's bachelor pad design didn't influence the size of the kitchen, which is enormous. When he met his wife, the kitchen's size became an international joke. 'Maliwan's mum is in Bangkok. There they produce huge amounts of food from a comparatively simple kitchen. When Maliwan showed her mother a picture of the kitchen, she burst out laughing and thought it was a restaurant. She couldn't believe you would need such a whopping stove,' he says. 'Now that I have a family, the kitchen gets used constantly. I'm much happier about that.'

Having Harry has modified Dare's lifestyle from high rev to a nicely paced hum. 'It's really amazing, the effect of a child. You end up hanging around the house a lot more. Now we prefer cooking at home to going out.'

MARCIA HOSKING LANDSCAPE DESIGNER

'WE STARTED OFF THINKING OF IT AS JUST A WEEKENDER,' SAYS LANDSCAPE DESIGNER MARCIA HOSKING. 'THEN WE BEGAN TO DREAM ABOUT HOW WE COULD LIVE HERE WHEN WE GOT OLDER – DO THE CHOOKS AND VEGIE GARDEN THING – AND ONCE THAT THOUGHT CRYSTALLISED, OUR APPROACH TO RENOVATING BECAME MORE SERIOUS.' THE IDYLLIC RETREAT THAT SHE SHARES WITH HER HUSBAND CHRIS, AN ARCHITECT, IS NESTLED IN A GREEN VALLEY A FEW HOURS SOUTH OF SYDNEY, IN THE SOUTHERN HIGHLANDS, AND HAS A SENSE OF FRENCH COUNTRY ABOUT IT.

Far left, a collection of ceramic jugs and old metal meatsafes in the pantry; **centre**, Marcia in the 'haphazardly planted' garden; **this page**, the colour of the living room walls was inspired by a visit to India. The doors open onto a side garden. Over the mantelpiece is a Kim Spooner painting titled *The Story of the Strange Waratah*.

Right, above the jugs in the pantry is a painting by Belinda Black, titled *Peas in a Pod*. Chris painted the wall with a tin of red woodwash he found on a road in Sydney; **below**, artist Kim Spooner's tamarillo painting stands atop an industrial cabinet which belongs to Marcia and Chris's daughter; **opposite page,** the Aga stove in the kitchen heats up the whole house.

'When we found the house, the things I loved about the property were the river nearby, the big oak tree and the old barn,' recounts Marcia. 'But the house! It was a flat-roofed, aluminium-windowed ugly duckling. We returned three weeks after we'd bought it and I thought, "What have we done?" Chris kept telling me he could turn this sow's ear into a silk purse. I have great faith in him, but I thought this would be a real test of that faith.'

As they pooled their creative minds, their plans continued to evolve. Visions of future grandchildren led them to consider a second storey. And that's when they found out the history of the old house.

'The dairy farmer who grazes cattle on our property told us that the house used to be sited on the other side of the river,' says Chris. 'It was originally a four-room timber cottage, with a verandah that ran around three sides of it.'

Marcia, a natural storyteller, takes over. 'Our neighbour, the farmer, used to ride past it on his horse on the way to school. The children who lived there always had health problems because the house was cold and dark, and eventually the wife put her foot down and said that the house had to be moved because it wasn't in the sun for long enough. Apparently they floated it across the river!'

After setting it on new foundations, the family continued to live there – hopefully enjoying better health than they had been. But some decades later, new owners decided to renovate and modernise. The steeply pitched roof was replaced with a flat roof spanning the four rooms and the verandah. Later, the verandah was bricked in and sliding aluminium windows were fitted.

Right, the master bedroom is a bright, feminine retreat; **below**, the tiles on the bathroom floor are from Vietnam, the vanity and bath surround are made from pigmented concrete; **opposite page**, the sunroom was originally enclosed by aluminium windows, which the couple replaced with timber. The painting on top of the industrial cupboard is another Kim Spooner, titled *Caress*.

'When we bought the house, it didn't look like an old house at all,' says Chris. 'There were obvious attempts to modernise it and all were poorly done or never properly resolved.'

But with a new pitched roof and picturesque dormer windows illuminating three upstairs bedrooms, the house again has a sweetness of form. Downstairs, the addition of a wide timber deck on the western side provides a space for gazing across paddocks dotted with black-and-white cows.

'I tried not to give in to the temptation to put great big panoramic-view windows everywhere,' says Chris. 'Framed views through windows and doors draw you outside. That's where we spend most of our time – out on the verandah.'

Directly inside is the heart of the house – a huge, eat-in kitchen, complete with a white-tiled nook, houses an Aga stove that heats the house in winter. Through a doorway is a sunny living room, with an adjacent sunroom (the old front verandah) painted a soothing eau de nil. At one end of the living room, French doors lead out into a sheltered easterly garden encircled by shrubs and taller trees.

'That was the other thing I loved about the place,' says Marcia. 'Being a landscape designer I could be a bit nitpicky about the design, but it was just beautifully done – haphazard but lovely.' She rolls off a list of mature trees, including two magnolias, a Chinese elm, a jacaranda and the oak.

'There are also some camellias in the side garden that provide me with flowers from winter through to early summer. I can always pick flowers in my garden. It's usually the first thing I do when I get here.'

JACKIE O RADIO PERSONALITY

'I LOVE GOING TO GALLERIES, BUT I'LL BE DAMNED IF I CAN AFFORD A WORK THAT SIZE,' SAYS GLAMOROUS RADIO STAR AND PART-TIME TV PRESENTER, JACKIE O. THE STRIKING TWO-BY-ONE METRE CANVAS IN HER APARTMENT LIVING ROOM SHOWS SHE HAS A TALENT FOR PAINTING AS WELL AS TALKING. JACKIE ESTIMATES THE POINTILLIST-STYLE PIECE, MADE UP OF THOUSANDS OF COLOURED DOTS, TOOK HER ABOUT 90 HOURS TO COMPLETE. 'IT WAS SO SATISFYING, BUT AFTER I FINISHED I THOUGHT, NEVER AGAIN. NEXT TIME I MIGHT JUST DO A WHITE CANVAS WITH A BIG BLACK STRIPE THROUGH IT!'

Far left, it took Jackie 90 hours to finish her dot painting, which now hangs in her living room; **centre**, Jackie in the park; **this page**, a chandelier bought in Prague hangs in the hallway of the completely revamped 1930s apartment.

Right, the living room is home to some of Jackie's timeless furniture, including the Coco lamp in the corner; **below**, Jackie's favourite colour, white, is used liberally in the bathroom; **opposite**, Jackie and Molly in the living room, where dark polished floorboards contrast with the light walls and airy windows.

Since Jackie and her English-born photographer husband Lee Henderson bought their two-bedroom 1930s second-floor apartment in the picturesque Sydney suburb of Elizabeth Bay, life has become more settled. Before that, radio work saw Jackie moving between Canberra, Adelaide and Melbourne. 'Elizabeth Bay is so beautiful because it's right next to the harbour and so close to Rushcutters Park,' she says. 'It's really peaceful here, but also just around the corner from Kings Cross, so you have the 24-hour convenience as well.'

The now predominantly white décor of the apartment is a drastic change from when they bought it. 'The transformation has been amazing,' she says of their renovations. 'Everything was different: the walls were rag-washed green and peach, the kitchen had multi-coloured cupboards, it was carpeted. We stayed within our $60,000 budget and got it done in six months by living in the lounge room.' Dark brown polished floorboards now provide a rich contrast with the white walls and woodwork. As does Jackie's large and dominating artwork.

She believes it's better to spend more on one piece that's timeless than to keep buying things to fit where you live. Her favourite pieces are a white Marcel Breur chair in the study, an egg lamp in the lounge, and Coco lamps in the bedroom and a corner of the lounge.

The item that's closest to her heart, however, is the chandelier in the hall, bought two years ago on a holiday in Prague. 'Chandeliers are so cheap there. We debated whether to bring it back, but in the end there was only one little piece damaged.'

DEAVER
Scott
PICASSO
JAS
MIN
MARIO TESTINO

JANE DE TELIGA FASHION DIRECTOR

'THE DOLLIES' HOUSE' IS HOW A MALE FRIEND ONCE DESCRIBED THE HOME OF JANE DE TELIGA, FASHION DIRECTOR OF THE AUSTRALIAN WOMEN'S WEEKLY. INDEED, THERE IS A WHISPER OF LITTLE WOMEN IN THE TERRACOTTA FEDERATION-ERA SEMI THAT JANE SHARES WITH HER TWO DAUGHTERS IN THE EASTERN SUBURBS OF SYDNEY. PRETTINESS ABOUNDS. BEYOND THE CREAM FRONT DOOR, A PASSAGE IS PAINTED PISTACHIO GREEN, AFTER THE MILAN SHOWROOM OF FASHION DESIGNER REBECCA MOSES. OFF TO THE RIGHT ARE TWO BEDROOMS, ONE OF WHICH IS PAINTED AN INCREDIBLY

Far left, the sitting room has jacaranda coloured walls and inherited 1930s tub chairs; **centre**, Jane de Teliga in her light-filled house; **this page**, tapestry cushions on the sitting room couch. The oil pastel of an interior is by Jane's sister, Sarah. The painted table is Indian.

JANE DE TELIGA

Right, as cupboard space is scarce, Jane makes the most of lavender storage boxes from Ikea; **below**, favourite fashion pieces hang over an imitation French armoire; **opposite page**, the bedroom, where Jane often retires to read and meditate, is a softly feminine place.

soft pink, with a powdery finish reminiscent of kalsomine.

The passage opens on to a jacaranda sitting room filled with natural sunlight that highlights the polished Baltic pine floorboards and woven tapestry rugs. The mantelpiece is covered with Art Deco glass tulips, paperweights, greeting cards by Kate de Kantzow, a small Buddha, chunks of amethyst and rose quartz, a ribbon painting by James Gordon, a Victorian nosegay and a pile of glistening mother-of-pearl pieces. Embroidered linen curtains, bought at a street market in Milan, billow in the breeze which comes through the French doors.

When it comes to decorating her home, Jane hankers after pieces from colonial India, is fascinated by Art Deco and prefers rooms with 'designated purposes', an attitude that belongs more to the 19th century than the 21st. 'I've never been one for banging holes in everything,' she says.

Her home reflects a taste for lovely things that leaves no room for minimalism. Favourite fashion pieces are used as decoration; caftans embellished with cutwork, appliqués from Joan Bowers, cross-cultural pieces by Easton Pearson, as well as heirlooms from the house of Jane's grandmother, who lived in Hunters Hill, and from the Federation house in Hornsby where she grew up with her parents and five siblings. 'We never have enough space, because we have lots of stuff. I can't control the papers, books, magazines – they take over my life,' she says, laughing.

Jane started her career as curator for the Art Gallery of New South Wales, a background that has served her well in putting passing trends into perspective. 'My home is a sanctuary from today's technology. I like it to be peaceful. It's where I disappear sometimes.'

JULIE PATERSON FABRIC DESIGNER

'I LIKE THE OLD THINGS THAT FEEL LIKE THEY'VE GOT HISTORY TO THEM,' SAYS FABRIC DESIGNER JULIE PATERSON. 'I DON'T LIKE NEW AND CLEAN. "OLD" CREATES A MORE COMFORTABLE AND RELAXED ENVIRONMENT.' MOVING THROUGH HER HOME IS LIKE GOING ON A SMALL DISCOVERY TOUR. HER APARTMENT NEAR THE BEACH IN SYDNEY'S COOGEE WAS PART OF ONE BIG HOUSE. 'IT WAS BUILT AT THE TURN OF THE CENTURY AND IN THE 1920S THEY CONVERTED IT INTO NINE FLATS. THEY'RE ALL DIFFERENT SHAPES AND SIZES AND THE BACK BLOCK USED TO BE STABLES.'

Far left, fox terrier Agnes Moorehead casts a critical eye over Julie Paterson's artwork in the orange hallway; **centre**, Julie at work in her studio/kitchen; **this page**, the living room. Julie took the wallpaper off and then decided to leave the wall markings as they were. The chair is from St Vincent de Paul.

JULIE PATERSON

Top row, left to right, Julie's artworks and fabrics set the tone in the living room. The floorboards are painted pale green; knick-knacks on a stool; the bedroom is host to Julie's love of rag rugs, crochet and colour. She hung the sheer curtains up for a cocktail party and they have stayed on. **Bottom row, right to left**, Julie and Agnes in the kitchen; a tiny display of art above the toilet; a bronze pig and a cowrie shell perch on top of one of Julie's paintings titled *Even*.

The original Victorian architecture includes high ceilings and thick, soundproof walls. Renovations and an extension in the 1950s added the now enclosed balcony bedroom as well as the powder-blue tiled kitchen and bathroom. 'The place has got a sense of those two eras,' says Julie.

The colour scheme of the living room and artworks is based on the muted green and dusky pink shades of the room's exposed plasterwork. She points to the walls in her living room. 'The colours in these walls have influenced everything, really,' she says. The walls have been painted with three tints of a colour Julie made up and calls Mimosa Yellow. Patches of the original wall, beautiful in their decay, are visible through 'windows' in the new paintwork.

The only major renovation Julie's done is to knock the wall through from the living room to the bedroom to catch the light. A clock, curtains and a bathroom cabinet hang off string, wire and original hooks. 'I'm the queen of botch jobs, I never get anyone in to help. It's quite a pragmatic approach really,' she says. 'I haven't got a drill, so I prop up my work instead of hanging it. I haven't got natural light in my studio, so I limit my colour palette, paint in bad light and see what effect it has!'

Her apartment is a reflection of the creative approach to her work where she dyes and prints colour and pattern onto natural, textured fabrics, creating home furnishings and clothing ranges. 'I chuck things together and mix them all up. I'm always moving things around until they find a home.'

NEIL PERRY RESTAURATEUR

NEIL PERRY PUT AUSTRALIA IN PRIME POSITION ON THE WORLD CULINARY MAP WHEN HE ESTABLISHED HIS SYDNEY RESTAURANT ROCKPOOL IN 1989. HE STILL HAS ROCKPOOL AND HE IS STILL BRIMMING WITH ENERGY, DEVISING NEW PROJECTS – A SIGNATURE RANGE OF PRODUCE FOR WOOLWORTHS SUPERMARKETS AND MENUS FOR QANTAS. THEN THERE'S THE FOURTH TELEVISION SERIES HE'S FINISHED FILMING FOR THE LIFESTYLE CHANNEL, AND A THIRD COOKBOOK WHICH HE HAS LAUNCHED. WHILE HE'S NOT SO FLAT OUT THAT HE'S IN DANGER OF NEGLECTING HIS TRADEMARK

Far left, some of the art on display through the house. The piece at the far end was created by tie-dying an old kimono, centre is an untitled work by Victorian artist, Esther Erlich, the black and white stick drawing is by New Zealand artist Jacqueline Fraser; **centre**, Neil and his wife, Samantha; **this page**, Neil's massive collection of cookbooks is partly kept on open shelves in the living room, but there are still 20 boxes of them in storage;

Right, Neil in his kitchen where everything is easily accessible; **below**, he designed the workbench and rack himself; **opposite page**, the bedroom's red and white colour scheme echoes the rest of the house.

ponytail (razor sharp and shiny), things are hectic enough for him to put off a game of golf with wife Samantha, who admits it's been a long time since they've had a typical weekend. 'We used to play golf and tennis, but now there's too much other stuff on,' she says from their home in Sydney's eastern suburbs, where they live with the newest member of the Perry clan, daughter Macy.

Time out for Neil Perry is about spending time with his family. Josephine, Neil's daughter from his first marriage, is often around on the weekends. Friday is dinner at home with a movie. Both Samantha and Neil cook, usually serving slow roasts or an easy pasta and salad with a bottle of red. 'This is a nice kitchen to work in,' says Neil, who built the workbench and rack for pans and kitchen aids.

On Saturday morning it's time to restock the pantry, so the family piles into the car for an excursion to visit some of the city's best providers. 'We love shopping for food and drinking wine,' says Neil. When they manage to catch up with friends, it's usually for an early Sunday lunch at home. 'By the weekend I just want to spend time with Sam, Josephine and Macy,' he says.

Artworks abound in their home. Above the dining table hangs an abstract painting by South Australian artist Keren Seelander. In the stairwell, there is a wall-hanging created from a kimono, as well as an untitled work by Victorian artist Esther Erlich and a black and white oilstick on paper by New Zealand artist Jacqueline Fraser. At the top of the stairs sits a Buddha statue. 'I love the philosophy of Buddhism. It's about how to lead your life, not about fearing God. It's a serene religion and I think it makes me a calmer person.'

LEONA EDMISTON FASHION DESIGNER

'WE WEREN'T LOOKING FOR A COUNTRY HOUSE,' SAYS FASHION DESIGNER LEONA EDMISTON, STANDING OUTSIDE HER 1860s WEATHERBOARD HOME, THE OLDEST DWELLING IN THE VILLAGE. 'ON OUR HONEYMOON 18 MONTHS AGO WE DECIDED TO DRIVE BACK TO SYDNEY FROM MELBOURNE VIA THE VILLAGES OF THE SOUTHERN HIGHLANDS. WE DROVE UP A QUIET LITTLE STREET AND CAME ACROSS THIS HOUSE – IT WAS FOR SALE. WE LOOKED AT THIS GORGEOUS PLACE, THEN AT EACH OTHER. THERE WAS ABSOLUTE SILENCE IN THE CAR – WE LOVED IT AND KNEW

Far left, Archie and Henry take a well-earned rest; **centre**, Leona Edmiston outside her weekend retreat; **this page**, a rattan sofa with soft comfortable cushions sets the tone for the house.

LEONA EDMISTON

Right, the kitchen where the couple cook for their stream of visitors; **below**, the glass-walled dining room with a 1950s dining setting; **opposite page,** Leona on a daybed. The colours and furniture have been chosen to create a tranquil space.

we had to buy it. We settled in eight days.' She and her husband, Jeremy Ducker, have cottoned on to the idea that the city is for working, while the country is for living. Their rural weekend retreat feels a lifetime away from Sydney, although it's only a 90-minute drive from their city base.

The house was nearly covered by the branches of a massive pine tree when they bought it. After pruning the tree, they decided to play with the interior by renovating the kitchen and bathroom, as well as the sunroom that runs along one side of the house.

Once the work was complete, they stuffed a truck full of furniture, paintings and books and drove down from Sydney. 'Our city place is Art Deco,' Leona explains, 'so it's exciting to have a different look here, although we were guided by the architecture a bit. I love the idea of an 1860s cottage filled with 1950s furniture – it looks fresh but not too heavy.'

The kitchen is full of found objects and second-hand pieces, and is the centre of activity. It opens to the glass-walled dining room where the couple's guests can dine and enjoy watching the mist roll in and envelop the house. The garden is also a source of much enjoyment. Apart from roses, Leona and Jeremy's garden also features lavender, wisteria, jasmine, camellias and hydrangeas. The garden falls away to a perfectly manicured lawn and features a huge magnolia tree and a cherry blossom.

Leona may have gone country but her desire for retail therapy hasn't diminished. She enjoys visiting the local antique stores that abound in the area. 'I love to spend a couple of hours browsing on the weekend,' Leona confesses. 'It's fabulous. Look at this – a lovely cup and saucer for only $6.50!'

IN THE HEART OF
PARIS

This page, glamorous feathered hats adorn the mantelpiece of the creamy bedroom; **opposite page**, the bathroom. Leona has had the artwork in the house framed simply.

AKIRA ISOGAWA FASHION DESIGNER

IF NOT FOR THE ODD DECORATIVE OBJECT AND LUXURIOUS FABRIC STREWN ABOUT, YOU MIGHT CALL AKIRA ISOGAWA'S STUDIO 'MONASTIC'. SITUATED IN A GLORIOUS OLD APARTMENT BLOCK IN SYDNEY'S INNER-CITY SUBURB OF DARLINGHURST, IT HAS THE DETAIL AND KIND OF SPACE AN ARTIST DREAMS OF CALLING HOME. 'IT'S BIGGER THAN ANY OTHER PLACE I'VE LIVED IN AND IT HAS HIGH CEILINGS, WHICH IS NICE,' HE SAYS. 'I THINK A HIGH CEILING IS VERY IMPORTANT. IT FREES UP YOUR SPIRIT.' WITHIN THE OCHRE YELLOW WALLS OF HIS APARTMENT, ALL THE ELEMENTS OF HIS DAILY LIFE ARE PLAIN

Far left, inspirational books on display; **centre**, Akira on the timber bed he designed and had made by a friend, the painting on the wall is a Korean watercolour of a tiger; **this page**, the main room. The designer loves the high ceilings of his ochre yellow rooms.

AKIRA ISOGAWA

'I don't have many things because I'm not good at managing them – I always lose them,' says Akira. **Right**, a table for two; **below**, the bedroom. Simplicity mixes with patterned fabrics and rich colour; **opposite page**, open shelves display the designer's essential reading.

to see: a bed, desk, two tables, two chairs and bookshelves. Although he has few possessions – not even a car – each one has a practical or aesthetic purpose. 'I don't have many things because I'm not good at managing them – I always lose them,' he says.

The deliberate and ordered arrangement of his furniture and belongings ensures Akira maintains the sense of space that's so important to him. He sleeps on a box-like timber bed he designed and had custom-made by a friend. Above it hangs a Korean watercolour of a tiger, one of a small collection of pictures that adorn the walls of the apartment. In the kitchen, a neat row of Japanese teacups and bowls sits on open shelves. 'I prefer to have everything visible so you know you are in control,' he admits. 'I hate to feel there's a few boxes in the corner and you don't know what's inside.'

Akira's sense of continuity clearly lies within his work, not in the ownership of objects. He often works seven days a week to keep up with his ever increasing workload. 'I'm looking forward to doing more work in the apartment,' he says. 'I've started bringing things here from the studio because I can be quite creative in this space.' And, for Akira, 'Creativity is evolution.'

The Art of Macramé
FRUITS
AUBREY BEARDSLEY
GREAT WORLD ATLAS
ISSEY MIYAKE
ISSEY MIYAKE East Meets West
OSCAR WILDE
Fashion
BELGIAN FASHION DESIGN
OTTOMAN EMBROIDERY
MOKUBA
FASHION
NEW FASHION JAPAN
METRIC PATTERN CUTTING
MODEL STORE

Left, a chair covered in Indian fabric and a cushion from a fashion show in Paris sits in the library; **below**, Jane in one of her favourite black and white combinations; **opposite page**, in the living room is an old Sydney bus roll and photos by Martyn Thompson. The cabinet is from Bali.

JANE ROARTY FASHION EDITOR

'I LOVE CLASHES AND I'M NOT AT ALL ANAL ABOUT MY HOUSE. IT'S LIKE A DRESS – I WEAR IT,' SAYS JANE ROARTY, EXECUTIVE FASHION EDITOR OF *MARIE CLAIRE*. HER CHARMING COTTAGE IN SYDNEY'S INNER-WEST IS THE PERFECT SPOT FOR A SELF-CONFESSED 'HOMEBODY' TO UNWIND AFTER DASHING ACROSS TIME ZONES TO KEEP UP WITH CHANGING TRENDS IN THE WORLD OF INTERNATIONAL FASHION. AN ABUNDANCE OF BEAUTIFUL OBJECTS COLLECTED DURING JANE'S NUMEROUS TRIPS OVERSEAS AND AN ASTUTE JUXTAPOSITION OF PATTERN, COLOUR AND TEXTURE CONFIRM HER STATUS

AND CUMBERLAND HIGH SCHOOL
AND DRUMMOYNE Av
AND LEICHHARDT DEPOT
AND RYDE DEPOT
RACECOURSE
SCHOOL
ROUND
CIAL
TH PARK
FIELD
RTS GROUNDS
RESS
PARK
TRIAL
ARTER
OU ENTER

Right, Jane's desk and window are covered in clashing Indian fabrics; **below**, striped pottery from Morocco sits on top of an antique Chinese cupboard; **opposite page**, the kitchen contains charcoal drawings of vegetables by Georgina Stroud and a French chandelier. On the table is some of Jane's collection of Pillivuyt French porcelain.

as one of the country's most sought-after arbiters of style.

'Everything's been done in the most simplistic way,' she says. 'It's about gradually collecting and adding personality, so that it keeps evolving.'

Jane says that fashion is 'in the blood'. Born and raised in Newcastle, north of Sydney, she spent many hours sitting with her mother (a successful dressmaker) and 'feeling the fabrics as she sewed beautiful ball gowns and wedding dresses'. This early encounter developed into something of a passion for pattern and texture, which can be seen throughout her home's interior. Jane's favourite room is the library, where bookcases lining two walls are filled with collections of cookbooks, and photography and fashion titles. Here limited-edition fine art is displayed on deep vermilion walls, which lend the space a meditative quality essential for the creative reflection required to track the pace of fashion.

She likes to fill the wall spaces with a range of framed pictures. 'Most of my art is photographs from mates,' she says. Above the sitting room couch hangs a trio of black-and-white photographs by her best friend, Martyn Thompson, including one that captures a poignant moment in her career. 'That's Linda Evangelista wearing a Philip Treacy hat,' says Jane, who styled the shoot in the early 1990s while she was a contributing editor of *Vogue Australia*.

Filling the house are fabrics collected overseas or bought from her friend Susie Middleton, who imports Indian textiles. And there are loads of quirky 'souvenirs': striped pottery from Marrakech, an old Sydney bus roll, and lampshades from Paris.

'The first thing I do when I'm in Paris for the collections is head to a

JANE ROARTY

Right, the living room. A portrait of supermodel Linda Evangelista by Martyn Thompson hangs over a sofa covered in Italian fabric; **below**, Jane in her bedroom with her beloved dogs, Maddie and Bernie. The walls are painted a dark brown she mixed herself; **opposite page**, the feature wall in the guest room is painted white and overlaid with yellow pigment stripes.

great hardware department store that [fashion writer] Maggie Alderson put me on to. Once I found these huge pink and apricot globes and I've scattered them all around the house. You have to adjust your eyes at night though,' she jokes, 'because the light is so diffuse.'

This includes her French chandelier, which hangs over the dining table. It's the antithesis to Jane's chalk-white kitchen. A passionate cook, this is her second-favourite room. The tongue-and-groove walls and cupboards are reminiscent of Nantucket beach houses, and charcoal drawings of vegetables by another friend, Georgina Stroud, are suspended above the windows.

On a tall wire unit, stacked in orderly rows, are pieces of Jane's greatest passion: Pillivuyt French porcelain. 'I've collected it since I was a girl and brought all the lidded soup bowls back from Paris,' she says. There's also a Daubière (covered pottery dish for cooking classic French stew), a Moroccan tagine and 'a true Sicilian pasta strainer'. She breaks up all that white with a colourful collection of French tablecloths. 'I also collect aprons from a little shop in Milan that sells maid's uniforms,' she says, adding, 'but I have to be careful or I'll end up with stockings and garters.'

Feature walls including a bright lime-coloured wall in the sitting room breaks up the otherwise white colour scheme, and in the guest bedroom a white wall has been overlaid with yellow pigment stripes, courtesy of her niece.

'I love people who express themselves and make an effort,' Jane says. And that goes for her home, too. Although she's a big fan of wearing basic black, she is the first to admit she could never, ever, be a minimalist.

Left, the dining room. The table is so old that it has grooves on the top from people's elbows, according to Eva; **below**, Eva and her daughter Kelly; **opposite page**, a baroque gilt mirror dominates the living room. The Howard piano was given to Eva by her parents when they arrived in Australia from Holland after World War II.

EVA HANNAH ARTIST

'BRIGHT AND EXUBERANT' BEST DESCRIBES PAINTER EVA HANNAH'S TWO-STOREY TERRACE HOUSE IN SYDNEY'S WOOLLAHRA AND HER SOUGHT-AFTER WORKS OF ART. HER HOME IS FILLED WITH A COLLECTION OF ANTIQUES, HEIRLOOMS AND PAINTINGS – MEMENTOS OF A RICH LIFE. WHEN SHE BOUGHT THE HOUSE ABOUT SIX YEARS AGO IT LOOKED VERY DIFFERENT. 'IT WAS A VERY DILAPIDATED SINGLE STOREY,' SAYS EVA. 'THERE WAS AN OLD WELL UNDER MY BEDROOM,' ADDS DAUGHTER KELLY, WHO SHARES HER MOTHER'S TALENTS AS WELL AS HER HOME. 'WE DISCOVERED THAT

Right, Kelly's bedroom. On the wall is *Kelly's Girls*, painted by the artist for her daughter; **below**, the painting on top of Eva's mother's sewing box was done by a boy who hid with her Jewish family in occupied Holland during the war. An antique telescope bought in Australia leans against the wall; **opposite page**, the Edwardian dresser in the living room is hand-painted. The pink and blue Murano glass figures are based on the cabaret dancers in *Kelly's Girls*. The antique clock was given to Eva by her late husband, Kevin.

when they started building,' continues Eva. 'The house took about two years to finish.'

What exists now is an airy, light-filled home that exudes all the charm of its inhabitants. Downstairs is Kelly's bedroom and a large living area that flows from kitchen to dining area to living room. Glass doors open up to take in the courtyard, which is filled with terracotta pots of lavender, azaleas and jasmine.

Upstairs is Eva's bedroom and her studio, where she works for most of the day producing paintings to exhibit and sell both here in Australia and overseas. Over a bed hangs one of Eva's paintings, *Kelly's Girls*, which became the inspiration for a series of glass *objets d'art* produced by a glass master on the Venetian island of Murano.

Everywhere in this charming home are pieces of family history – leather-bound dictionaries that belonged to Eva's parents, paintings that Kelly has produced since she quit a stressful career and took up art herself and, on top of a dresser in the living room, a collection of heirloom silverware. Above that sits a large, ornate French clock given to Eva by her late husband, Kevin. 'It's never worked,' says Eva. 'My father was a watchmaker, but the clock is so heavy he could never easily work on it.'

One of the more amazing stories is about a painting, one of the few not painted by Eva or Kelly. As a small child, Eva lived in Holland and when World War II erupted, her family, who are Jewish, went into hiding. 'The people who housed us looked after many people,' she says, 'and this was painted by one of the boys who was hidden there. I took my girls to visit him when they were children and he gave us that painting.'

BAR

ZAHAVA ELENBERG ARCHITECT

'WE REALLY LIKED THE IDEA OF LIVING AND WORKING IN THE SAME PLACE,' SAYS ARCHITECT ZAHAVA ELENBERG. THE CONVERTED WAREHOUSE SHE SHARES WITH HUSBAND AND BUSINESS PARTNER CALLUM FRASER PROVIDES THEM WITH EVERYTHING THEY NEED: A HOME, OFFICE, AND SHOWROOM TO PROMOTE THEIR BUSINESS, MOVE-IN, A COMPLETE FURNISHING SERVICE FOR HOMES AND INVESTMENT PROPERTIES. 'IT WAS REGARDED AS THE UGLIEST BUILDING IN THE AREA,' SHE SAYS OF THE 1960s FORMER TEXTILE LAMINATING FACTORY IN MELBOURNE'S INNER-CITY SUBURB OF FITZROY.

Far left, a drawing by Akio Makigawa sits on top of the white cupboard, the wooden bunny is by Emily Floyd; **centre**, Zahava in front of a painting by Gary Wilson; **this page**, the living section has eight-metre-long shelves containing the 'mobile library'.

ZAHAVA ELENBERG

Right, the dining area. Many of the art pieces come from the Anna Schwartz gallery owned by Zahava's mother. Zahava's late father, Joel Elenberg, sculpted the bronze head.

'But we thought it was so beautiful structurally, we could see how it would work as a home and office.'

The two-storey warehouse was ideal for their ambitious undertaking. The ground floor became the Move-in showroom with garages alongside it and the upstairs became a two-bedroom apartment and the office of their architectural business, Elenberg Fraser, each with a separate entrance at street level. The upstairs layout also allows for more converted office space when the business expands.

From the outside, little has changed, except that there's substantially more glazing than ever before. In addition, a hole was punched through the building on the west side to frame the large windows of the new office. At ground level, a shopfront window now tempts passers-by with a selection of Move-in's contemporary furnishings.

Internally, the factory was gutted, with most pre-existing walls removed to accommodate the new configuration. Upstairs Zahava and Callum wanted the design kept 'robust and simple' in keeping with the fabric of the old factory. The 250-square-metre apartment is testament to this streamlined approach. With the kitchen's large stainless-steel bench forming the 'centrepiece', the apartment's only proper rooms are at either end: the couple's bedroom with walk-in robe and a bathroom on one side, and their daughter's room on the other. Beside the kitchen is a staircase leading to a mezzanine floor that's entirely devoted to storage, keeping the downstairs area blissfully free of clutter. At the living-room end of the apartment is an eight-metre-long 'mobile library', as Zahava calls it, because 'the books are constantly moving between home and office'.

Right, in the walk-in wardrobe is a Zig Zag chair by Rietveld; **below**, Zahava and Callum's bedroom; **opposite page**, in another corner of the bedroom is a Mies van der Rohe recliner. The small bronze in the hallway is by Joel Elenberg.

Retaining the original factory floor has made it a permanent reminder of the building's past. 'The floor has a history and a pattern of splashes and dents running through it that we wanted to keep, so we didn't even grind it back – just coated the whole thing with a high-gloss polyurethane,' she says.

Similarly, the vaulted ceiling was left exposed, unashamedly displaying the waterproof silver sarking beneath the corrugated-iron roof. High windows keep the apartment drenched in sunlight, and a commercial air-conditioning system alleviates any concerns about the iron roof and muggy Melbourne summers. However, according to Zahava, the roof has one disadvantage: 'When it rains heavily, it's too loud to speak on the phone!'

Artificial lighting is one of the few defining factors in the large open space. Industrial-strength pendant lights dangle high above the dining table and island bench, while the living room has downlights that can be dimmed and spotlights strategically placed to highlight the couple's prized collection of art. 'My mother has a contemporary gallery and I've grown up in that world, so Callum and I have always been keen collectors of pieces from our own generation,' says Zahava, who admits they succumb to buying at least one large artwork every year.

Zahava finds their warehouse conversion particularly conducive to running the businesses and looking after the couple's daughter. 'It's so much easier when you can flit between home and work,' she adds. With their business and home life in one ordered location, the duo have turned travel time into the minute it takes them to trip up or down the stairs.

Left, avocado walls make a glowing backdrop for tribal art; **below**, Gabrielle's love of colour is evident throughout the house; **opposite page,** fresh magnolia blossoms mirror *Unravel*, one of Gabrielle's paintings. The wooden bowls are from Papua New Guinea.

GABRIELLE COURTENAY ARTIST

'WE WANTED A SILK FINISH ON A POLYESTER BUDGET,' SAYS GABRIELLE COURTENAY, LAUGHING. 'THAT WAS IT BASICALLY. WE WANTED IT VERY SIMPLE.' GABRIELLE'S RENOVATED HOME IN SYDNEY'S EASTERN SUBURBS IS COMPELLING EVIDENCE OF HER INTUITIVE GIFT FOR COLOUR. SHE AND PARTNER GREGORY SMITH, TOGETHER WITH ARCHITECT ROBERT WEIR, POOLED THEIR CREATIVE TALENTS TO CREATE A STYLISH RENOVATION THAT DIDN'T COST THE EARTH. SHE CHOSE THE COLOURS AND PAINTED THE HOUSE; GREGORY, A TRAINED SCULPTOR, WHO CREATES ARCHITECTURAL

Right, in the second storey studio/TV room a Timorese sculpture watches over a chair and teak sideboard from the 1960s; **below**, the sculptural staircase makes a statement against the purple-brown walls of the ground floor; **opposite page**, Gabrielle mixed the deep watermelon red on the walls of the master bedroom herself. Above the bed is *Vanilla*, another of her paintings.

features and finishes, designed the striking staircase and kitchen, and also helped paint; while Robert focused on space and planning issues.

Within the house, Gabrielle's rich, earth-bound colours create a warm environment filled with tribal sculpture collected in Papua New Guinea, mixed with contemporary art, antiques and modern classics – all pulled together by the unerring eye of an artist against a backdrop of strong colour.

The house's transformation is a long way from the drab and dingy semi it used to be. 'It was a three-bedroom 1930s house, closed in and dark,' says Gabrielle. 'We lived here for 10 years before we did anything, but we needed more light and space.'

She had raised two children in the house, but now that both are grown up, she and Gregory wanted a separate zone for themselves and one for the kids, which they could eventually rent out. The answer was simple: a new second storey with a loft space that would be the parents' zone. The original front of the house at ground level – comprising two bedrooms, a bathroom and laundry – is left to the kids.

Upstairs a balcony overlooks the backyard, a lush, semi-tropical oasis that Gabrielle describes as 'our own little hideaway'.

On the rear ground floor, the living room, kitchen, laundry and third bedroom were reconfigured into a single, open-plan living space that looks out on the garden. Dominated by the sculptural staircase, it's the scene for many a gathering. 'It's great having the deck on the same level,' she says. 'When we throw a party, we simply pull the sofas out onto the deck. We love being here. The whole place is fresher and lighter.'

LYN GARDENER VINTAGE-STORE OWNER

'I WANTED A FEMININE HOME, WITH SOFT, BEAUTIFUL FADED FABRICS. I WANTED ROOMS FULL OF CHANDELIERS. MY HOME IS A REALLY GOOD INTERPRETATION OF WHAT MY SHOP IS ALL ABOUT,' SAYS LYN GARDENER, OWNER OF MELBOURNE VINTAGE STORE EMPIRE 111. NOW A VISION IN WHITE, HER LUXURIOUS DOUBLE-STOREY INNER-CITY TERRACE WAS ONCE A RUN-DOWN WAREHOUSE. 'IT WAS A DARK, DINGY OLD MATTRESS FACTORY WITH DIRTY OLD CONCRETE, ASBESTOS AND NO LIGHT,' SHE SAYS. 'THERE WERE BROKEN FLOORBOARDS UPSTAIRS AND HOLES IN THE ROOF.'

Far left, mirrors reflect light in the living room; **centre**, Lyn with some of her collection of vintage quilts and clothing; **this page**, the dining area had all internal walls removed. The lower half of the windows is translucent to bring in light but keep a sense of privacy.

Right, Lyn's love of vintage is evident throughout the house – chandeliers and dresses decorate the bathroom; **below**, faded floral quilts are stacked in a cupboard; **opposite page**, Lyn's favourite place, the bedroom, features an original cast-iron claw-foot bath which she soaks in for hours.

And yet, when it became available for sale, she jumped. 'I love homes that are broken down. If it was already done up, I would feel like I couldn't change it. I know what I want, and it's got to be exactly that.' The idea of doing such a massive overhaul was anything but daunting. 'It was a really good challenge,' she says.

Lyn's instincts were right. After just four months' work, she has transformed the dilapidated building into a light and bright sanctuary which mixes her love of all things yesteryear with a contemporary flair. Although many of the pieces in her home are vintage, there is a feeling of modernity throughout the space. That, she explains, is because 'it's so fresh – the colour makes such a big difference'.

Overlapping hues – the walls are painted ivory, while a daybed is more alabaster – serve to create depth. A collection of pearly 'milk glass' lines her kitchen shelves, crystal chandeliers hang haphazardly from the ceiling, and the outside view of snowy-white concrete is slowly disappearing amidst the greenery of climbing roses.

An aura of luxury pervades this abode, partly through the small treasures such as handmade 1950s boxes, beaded vintage gloves and ornate hairpieces that lie around in odd corners. Then there is the way Lyn lives her life – she'll sleep, for example, in something from her collection of 1930s and '40s peignoirs. 'I love being in bed in my favourite slip-nightie, even though no-one's there to see it. I live my passion. I take vintage living to the nth degree.'

AMANDA BRISKIN FOUNDER OF MIMCO

WHEN YOU WALK INTO AMANDA BRISKIN'S HOME, IT'S NOT IMMEDIATELY APPARENT THAT SHE'S THE ENTREPRENEUR BEHIND SUCCESSFUL ACCESSORIES COMPANY MIMCO. SURE, THERE'S A SWATCH OF FLORENCE BROADHURST WALLPAPER ON A TABLE, BUT YOU'RE MORE LIKELY TO SEE LEGO SCATTERED ACROSS THE CARPET AND HEAR THE SOUND OF CHILDREN AT PLAY. FOR AMANDA AND HUSBAND DAVID, BOTH DIRECTORS OF MIMCO, HOME IS WHERE THEY HANG OUT WITH THEIR SONS, BLAKE AND INDIANA. THEIR FOUR-BEDROOM, OPEN-PLAN HOUSE IN THE MELBOURNE

Far left, Amanda Briskin loves to forage through markets for finds like this vintage glass bowl; **centre**, Amanda in her office; **this page**, the hallway features a bronze Moroccan urn and a glimpse of Amanda's large glass collection.

Right, the bathroom. Amanda's more unusual jewellery finds are hooked onto a suede-backed board; **below**, in the front courtyard the stone sculpture is from Bali; **opposite page**, the silvery wallpaper in the bedroom makes a romantic backdrop for the upholstered leather bedside table.

suburb of Caulfield incorporates comfortable rooms that aren't at all precious, even while showcasing her impressive array of collectables. Many pieces have been picked up all over the world. Amanda admits that on occasion she has paid more in excess luggage charges than for the items themselves. One of these, a stone Buddha sculpture from Bali, is displayed prominently in her front courtyard, where stone and pebble landscaping add to the Asian feel. Another memento, a large Moroccan bronze urn, is featured in the hallway in full view of the polished jarrah staircase.

Amanda finds vintage vases and glass bowls irresistible and these are displayed in many of the rooms. The bar, where the couple entertain, is where most of her Murano glass is kept. Wallpaper is another theme: wallpaper prints found at London's Spitalfield's Market hang as artwork and floral wallpaper creates a soothing atmosphere in their bedroom, where Amanda says she loves to lounge on the weekends.

With the office situated at the back of the house, it takes some discipline to stick to weekday hours. 'When we started our business, it was harder to keep our weekends separate from work. Since then, we've learned how to switch off,' says Amanda. A large floral wall tapestry in the office brings the feel of the garden, as seen through the glass doors, inside.

When there's an opportunity on the weekend, she will fit in a bit of window shopping. 'I'll either go to St Kilda or Brunswick. I love going to bits-and-pieces stores, seeing the way they accumulate things. I've bought a collection of glass genie bottles, both for the store and home. We've also got an upholstered green chair from there. I'll often pick up vases or even old coathangers, pegs, hooks or tins.'

THEFASHIC

SIMMONE LOGUE PROVIDORE

LIKE MANY COUNTRY HOUSES, ESSINGTON PARK CREAKS AND GROANS WITH THE BURDENS OF TIME. RUSTIC AND RATHER GOTHIC IN STYLE, IT IS SITUATED IN OBERON, TWO AND A BIT HOURS WEST OF SYDNEY, AND IS HOME TO TWIN SISTERS SIMMONE AND JOANNA (JOEY) LOGUE. 'ESSINGTON PARK WASN'T REALLY PART OF MY LONG-TERM PLAN, BUT WHEN WE SAW THE HOUSE WE FELL IN LOVE WITH IT AND JUST HAD TO BUY IT,' SAYS SIMMONE, WHO IS WELL KNOWN FOR HER RANGE OF DELECTABLE FINE FOODS. 'THE HOUSE WAS IN TERRIBLE DISREPAIR, BUT IT DIDN'T MATTER,'

Far left, an old table found by a friend holds an enamel jug filled with leaves from the garden; **centre,** Simmone on the verandah; **this page**, the old kitchen table is the setting for endless cups of tea and meals with family and friends.

SIMMONE LOGUE

Right, the pantry where seasonal produce is preserved and stored; **below**, Simmone calls the living room 'the nook' and has created a cosy mix of deep sofas and velvet curtains; **opposite page**, the bath, which was found in a paddock on the property, was re-enamelled and painted a rich dark grey.

'We saw a vision of life that had real meaning for us. It was a place for us to look after friends and family, feed them good home-cooked meals and provide a place for rest and repose. More than that, it was somewhere Joey could paint.'

Essington Park was built in 1860 and when the sisters took over as ladies of the manor they stripped away layers of history. 'We removed paint and junk from the 19th century and tore away blue velvet wallpaper and copper gargoyles from the 1970s,' says Simmone. They scrubbed bricks, painted walls and furnished the house with an unusual mix of antiques and objects they'd collected over the years.

The enormous kitchen is the life and soul of the house. 'During the winter it's very cold in Oberon, so we inevitably spend most of our time in the kitchen with our hands in front of the stove,' Simmone says. The stove, an old Metters, is one of her favourite things. 'You'd think I'd want to escape from food,' she continues. 'But I love to cook and enjoy preparing meals and making sure everyone is nourished and nurtured.'

Now the home is everything you'd want from a country estate: a ramshackle beauty that is both elegant and cosy. 'We've put a lot of energy into making it beautiful,' says Simmone. 'We've also tended the garden so that it's a playground for the dogs, donkeys and our extended family of friends.'

DONALD CAMPBELL INTERIOR DESIGNER

YOU WOULD EXPECT DONALD CAMPBELL, A SYDNEY-BASED DESIGNER OF INTERIORS AND TEXTILES, TO HAVE AN EYE AND FEEL FOR INTERIORS – AND HE DOES EXUDE A CERTAIN 'KNOWINGNESS' ON MATTERS OF STYLE, WHETHER HE'S IN HIS WEEKENDER ON PITTWATER OR IN HIS STYLISH CITY PAD. BOTH HOUSES SPEAK OF AN OWNER WITH ECLECTIC TASTES, A LOVE OF TEXTURES AND AN ABILITY TO THROW THINGS TOGETHER AND MAKE THEM WORK, WHETHER THEY ARE COLLECTIONS OF MODERN CLASSIC FURNITURE, OR DETRITUS COLLECTED FROM THE GARDEN AND THE BEACH.

Far left, a Danish sideboard in Donald Campbell's weekender holds Peter Fay's orange cup with yellow balls titled *Sun Up 2000*; **centre**, Donald against the original walnut veneer; **this page**, in the living room a 1950s aesthetic prevails with a tiled Danish table and period lounge.

The beach house. **Right,** a collection of feathered finds hangs outside the bedroom door; **below**, shells and seahorses gathered from the beach are laid out in a box; **opposite page**, the driftwood sculpture over the fireplace was made by Eliezer Zeev.

THE BEACH HOUSE Owning a beach house was the last thing on Donald's mind when, in late 2000, he took a water taxi to spend a weekend with friends who lived in Pittwater. He fell in love with the area and six months later he bought a property a few doors down from his hosts.

Rough stone steps meander up from the beach to the box-like 1960s structure. Donald thought it 'only needed cleaning and painting' until he swept the roof with a stiff-bristled broom and it rained: 'I'd popped every bit of rust and it was like living in a shower room. I had to renovate.'

He also wanted to extend the pole-supported deck on three sides of the house, and build a smaller one on a rock shelf below it. Now furnished with a table setting and even power points, the latter is a beguiling place for breakfasts and early-evening drinks. Against the advice of friends, he kept the walnut veneer on the living room walls because he thought the timber was 'cool'. The radiata pine floorboards were also retained, despite their condition. 'Someone had used acrylic-based varnish over oil-based varnish. It was peeling off and looked like fish scales all over the floor.' Donald grimaces. The remedy? It was stripped first and maintained with a sympathetic soap wash like one his grandmother had used.

As a strong believer in functional design, Donald is well pleased with the calm environment he's achieved. 'I grew up in a 1950s house where there wasn't good spatial organisation,' he says. 'The kitchen had a table in the middle and cupboards around the outside. Whenever someone walked between the chair and the cupboard, you had to move your chair out of the way. That sort of irritation made everyone involved tense. I realised that if you have clear, workable spaces, then the tension goes.'

BELL

The city house. **Right**, 'curtain walls' divide the apartment. In the entrance to the bedroom is a Womb chair and matching footstool by Eero Saarinen; **below**, a contemplative Donald at his desk. The painting behind him is *Black + Black + Black* by Lindy Lee; **opposite page**, a mix of artworks and modern furniture give the living room its urban edge. The red artwork is *Surf or Die* by Scott Redford, a huge Bill Henson work leans against the wall behind chrome chairs covered in white leather by Marcel Breuer.

THE CITY HOUSE Mirrored walls and a panoramic view of Sydney Harbour fill Donald Campbell's Sydney home with a sense of infinite space. This contemporary abode reflects a strong sense of aesthetics: it is clean without being hard, and light without being clinical.

But Donald's creative talents almost failed him during his first inspection of the classic 1958 apartment. 'It was filled with Corinthian columns that weren't properly installed,' he says, pulling a face. 'They were purely decorative and actually wobbled.' The original interior also included off-white shag pile, betraying roots of acid orange and yellow; an intricate series of dark corridors coated with hairy hessian wallpaper, given a 'second life' with coats of white paint; and dust-laden satin curtains shrouding the view of Sydney Harbour below. 'I looked around and thought, "No way!"' he says.

Less daunted on a second visit, he saw its potential. Two elements of the architecture gave the apartment an attractive edge on earlier periods of design. First, its aspect – a north-westerly one designed for maximum exposure to the afternoon sun. The second trump card was the presence of non-load bearing walls, allowing the space inside to be rearranged. He devised a plan to maximise the view on the harbour side of the apartment. By shortening some walls and removing others, the entrance foyer and dining area were connected to become a central space leading to the kitchen and bathroom. Two small office/relaxation spaces requiring less light were tucked in at the 'back' of the apartment, leading off on either side of the entrance foyer.

A freestanding, floor-to-ceiling dividing wall, originally built for Donald's

DONALD CAMPBELL

Right, a Sori Yanagi butterfly stool bought in Tokyo sits quietly under *Love Apples* by Rosalie Gascoigne; **below**, mirrors used to extend the space in the bedroom reflect an 18th-century tapestry and Lindy Lee's *Of Voluntary Death*; **opposite page**, a Warhol mural of Marilyn Monroe in the dining room. The chairs around the tables are by Charles and Ray Eames.

last abode, has been moved to this one and fitted with a series of built-in shelves and sliding doors. Inside, he stores the kind of treasured bric-a-brac – porcelain teacups and saucers and fine Austrian glassware – that would 'ruin the line', the kind that other people might have on display as decoration.

The mirrored walls at both ends of the central space create a familiar impression to those who grew up in a 50s house, complete with a patio. 'In a certain way, you want to have what you came from,' says Donald. 'Although I thought of myself as a lover of Victorian houses, when I moved here I realised I didn't actually like living in a house full of tiny rooms and different levels. I like high ceilings, but ground-level space is more important.' The walls are painted in a shade of white that works perfectly with his striking collection of 20th-century artworks and mid-century modern furniture.

The 'rightness' he was chasing in his interior was achieved by restraint, avoiding sentimental detours into retro. The 1948 dining table by Charles and Ray Eames and portraits of Marilyn Monroe by Andy Warhol had the 'it' factor, as did the Chinese side table and an eccentric art piece – a Perspex box containing a wedding dress.

A minimalist aesthetic is an undeniable influence, but Donald feels it's an intrinsic part of the Australian style that has only recently been picked elsewhere. 'New Yorkers are a bit shocked at our modernism. "How stark," they remark. "You couldn't possibly do such-and-such." But we've been doing it this way for 30 years.'

LEE MATHEWS FASHION DESIGNER

'I HADN'T CHECKED ON IT BEFORE WE MOVED IN AND WHEN WE GOT THERE IT DEFIED DESCRIPTION,' RECALLS LEE MATHEWS OF HER 1920s WEATHERBOARD COTTAGE. 'IT WAS SO UNLOVED AND DEPRESSING, I JUST CRIED.' POSITIONED HIGH ON A HILL AND SURROUNDED BY NATIONAL PARK, THE COTTAGE WHICH LEE SHARES WITH HER FAMILY OVERLOOKS PITTWATER, ON SYDNEY'S NORTHERN PENINSULA. FAUX-WOOD CONCRETE FURNITURE, SCULPTED ANIMALS AND UNATTENDED GRAPE VINES SUGGEST IT MAY HAVE ONCE BEEN A HOLIDAY HOUSE OR THE HOME OF A

Far left, a grand piano stands at one end of Lee Mathews's living room. The two chairs are covered in reproduction toile de Versailles fabric; **centre**, Lee in casual mode; **this page**, the bright pink fireplace dominates the living room. The painting on the left was bought at an auction.

Right, Lee and her son, Charlie, sit at the kitchen table which was made by Guy. Lee drew the cow painting on the wall; **below**, an old chair reflects Lee's 'nanna' style; **opposite page**, a corner of the guest room is a microcosm of the house's style with vintage finds and soft colours. A bench is piled high with quilts and handmade dolls. The silhouette of Guy was painted by Lee.

wine-maker. When Lee first saw it, years of rental occupants had taken their toll, leaving the cottage cracked and trembling from neglect. The decision to rent the property, let alone stay in it, was hardly rational, but Lee and husband Guy, a furniture maker and seller, saw its potential and had the skills to turn it into something special.

'He's good at making a silk purse out of a sow's ear,' says Lee. Guy's extensive experience restoring semi-industrial furniture and creating custom-made pieces for his own business has come in handy. 'Every year we do a patch-up job on this, that and the other to get us through to the next year, thinking we've got to move after this, but we can't because it's such an amazing place,' she says.

Many of the 'patch-ups' they've done have come via the leftover paint tins that Guy has stashed in the garage. When Lee looks at the green-over-cream stripes on the outside of the house, she grins, saying: 'I think that was as much green as Guy had left in the tin, so he made it stripes.'

Paint has been used to transform the interior of the home also. 'When we moved in, every wall was a smoky green colour, which works in the living room because it blends with the eucalypt-tree backdrop outside. We just painted the back wall five shades lighter than the others and it brightened everything.'

A former graphic designer who now hand-dyes her fabrics, Lee's preoccupation is colour. In the kitchen, she points to where the 'revolting biscuit colour' has been replaced with yellow, a pink feature wall and touches of mint. In the bedroom, Lee insisted on white. 'Colour in a bedroom disturbs me – I can't sleep,' she says. Meanwhile, the presently

8

LEE MATHEWS

Right, Lee's dresses hang on display throughout the house; **below**, old business signs decorate the wall between the kitchen and living rooms. The 1950s Cyclops pedal car makes a handy box holder; **opposite page**, the beds in the children's bedroom were originally used in a hospital.

pink fireplace has become the surface on which Guy and Lee continually experiment with colour.

'The house has entirely dictated what we've put in it,' she says, explaining how in recent years she has developed a 'nanna style' that draws on childhood memories of helping her seamstress grandmother. Her kitchen shelves are lined with zigzag-edged newspaper and every spare surface is covered with something cushioned, quilted or embroidered. This style has only intensified since she became a mother. The children's bedroom, Lee's favourite space, echoes the past with paintings of animals as well as hospital beds that date from her grandparents' era.

A counterbalance to Lee's cushioned chaos is Guy's need for clarity. He may use signs found at auctions as artworks and collect zinc letters to hang about the place, but there is order in the way he goes about it. 'Every time something comes in, something goes out,' says Lee. 'Once every few months he'll have a massive clean-up and all the junk will go away. Then I start to nervously pull things out and redecorate.'

What unifies their contrasting styles is a shared love for all things old – Lee guesses the only new things in the house are cooking utensils and sheets. And then, of course, there's the house itself. 'Whoever built it was very clever. There are lots of ways in and out of it and on to the balcony – no hallways.'

The biggest influence on Lee and Guy though has been the view from the front. 'Living in a national park and having to hike up through the garden to the house definitely changes how you start and finish your day,' Lee reflects. 'I don't think I could live any other way.'

K
KOOKABURRA

STEPHEN JOLSON ARCHITECT

A COMMENT FROM AN EX-GIRLFRIEND THAT HIS RENOVATED HOME WAS COLD AND TYPICAL OF A 'BOY'S HOUSE' PROMPTED MELBOURNE ARCHITECT STEPHEN JOLSON TO TRY AGAIN. 'IT'S NOT JUST HOW A RENOVATION LOOKS,' HE SAYS. 'IT'S HOW IT FUNCTIONS AND RELATES TO EVERYTHING, INCLUDING THE SUBTLE CHANGES OF LIGHT.' WHEN HE EMBARKED ON THE FIRST OF TWO RENOVATIONS OF HIS TWO-BEDROOM 1930S HOUSE IN PRAHRAN, IT FEATURED ALL THE HALLMARKS OF ITS PERIOD – A TERRACOTTA-TILED ROOF, EXPOSED RED-BRICK WALLS AND A TURNED-TIMBER VERANDAH.

Far left, though he's a bit of a minimalist, Stephen Jolson likes clusters of things. In this case a photo he took of a Tunisian desert nomad acts as a backdrop for some treasures; **centre**, Stephen in his twice-renovated house; **this page**, in the kitchen the 17th-century French table is on loan from his parents. The vase holds a collection of hand-blown straws.

STEPHEN JOLSON

Right, the large tin bowl on the dining table is from Tunisia, the lanterns came from Morocco. Stephen built the floor-to-ceiling cabinets behind the table for storing the more utilitarian aspects of the kitchen; **below**, the main bedroom. Stephen designed the bed and side tables. On the walls are photos he took in Egypt; **opposite page**, a steel screen with laser cut patterns was installed in the central courtyard, behind it is the bedroom. In the main living room is an original Le Corbusier chaise longue which belonged to Stephen's grandfather. The tables are made from rain drums bought in Cambodia.

the exterior was relatively intact, but the interior space had been carved into five box-sized rooms. Although the backyard was generous, its dimensions couldn't be appreciated – a caravan, doubling as an extra room, was left just outside the back door.

'There's nothing I liked about the original house,' says Stephen. 'It certainly wasn't the orientation [a south-facing garden]. The only good thing was the depth of the site [40 metres].' With the help of friends, he removed the stained carpet and several interior walls, which opened up the space. But after the remark from the ex-girlfriend, he embarked on the second phase, done on a limited budget, which included renovating the bathroom and converting the front room, originally a bedroom, to a home theatre.

Lined with artefacts and photos taken by Stephen on his travels to north Africa, South America and Asia, the rooms are animated, though uncluttered. India proved an inspiration for the laser-cut steel screen that veils Stephen's bedroom and ensuite. 'I was visiting a temple,' he remembers. 'The screen was in the middle of a courtyard, and it offered a sense of mysticism as well as curiosity.' In the same site is an angled water wall which uses recycled water and, along with a wall of Timor black bamboo Stephen planted, suggests the feeling of a tropical grotto. The idea of a house which connected to its exterior space was important to him.

It's hard to imagine a house so rich in detail, photos and objects would still be derided as typically boyish. But it's the architecture which makes it all work. 'This house was really designed as a blank canvas,' Stephen says. 'I like the idea that if everything was removed, it would still give me the same pleasure.'

JACQUELINE COATES ARTIST

WHEN JACQUELINE COATES PACKED HER BAGS AND ANNOUNCED SHE WAS MOVING TO A LITTLE TOWN IN SOUTH AUSTRALIA'S CLARE VALLEY, HER FRIENDS AND FAMILY WERE INCREDULOUS. HOW COULD THE GIRL THEY KNEW – AN ART DIRECTOR WHO LOVED THE BUZZ OF CITY LIFE AND HAD ALREADY CALLED SINGAPORE, MELBOURNE AND SYDNEY HOME – BE MOVING TO A PLACE CALLED KAPUNDA? 'I NEEDED TO PAINT!' SHE SQUEALS IN MOCK EXASPERATION. JACQUELINE FOUND THE 19TH-CENTURY, BLUESTONE-WALLED BARN BY CHANCE SIX YEARS AGO WHEN WORK

Far left, one of Jacqueline Coates's paintings hangs over a stone-topped antique washstand; **centre**, Jacqueline with Hannibal and Lily; **this page**, the living area is dominated by one of Jacqueline's flower paintings. The vinyl suite was bought at a garage sale.

JACQUELINE COATES

Right Jacqueline's children refer to this as the 'elephant couch' because it reminds them of the seats elephant riders use. Above it is *Hay Bales, Kapunda*. The yellow patchwork cushion was made by a friend; **below**, Hannibal sits next to a reproduction soft drink crate chest of drawers found in Byron Bay; **opposite page**, the children's room. The hand-knitted blankets were bought locally.

took her to Adelaide and Kapunda, an hour and a half north of the city. 'It looked a bit derelict, but also beautiful,' she explains. Then, when she was negotiating to buy the property, she met the man who would become the father of her children.

Three emotionally turbulent years later, in the heat of summer 2001, she moved to South Australia. Her barn was still uninhabitable and the little family stayed at nearby Anlaby Station while Jacqueline supervised the renovations. 'Frankly, this period was a nightmare, the hardest thing I've ever done. Yet at the same time it really felt right.' On the plus side, her paintings were starting to sell well and she had plenty of commissions.

Her brother, Nigel, a builder, stepped in to help draw up the new home's specifications. His first impressions were less romantic than hers. 'Unbelievable!' he says. 'I thought it was about to fall down!' The roof needed re-pitching and the eaves extended to keep rainfall off the walls. 'There was no drainage, no footings to speak of,' he explains. The stonework also had to be repainted. None of this deterred the owner.

Now the kitchen stands where a ground-level cow shed used to be, and the living area is where horses were once stabled. 'Upstairs, you can see the little hatches where they dropped the hay down to feed the horses,' she says. The cobbled floor has been levelled and the bluestones relaid horizontally, another of Nigel's clever ideas. Jacqueline paints in the studio between 10am and 4pm while the children are at daycare, as well as holding one-day workshops. The giant blooms that inspired her to move are gradually being joined by new subjects – hay bales, plants, figs, quinces, apples on boughs and pumpkins – that reflect her new life.

DEBORAH HUTTON MEDIA PERSONALITY

DEBORAH HUTTON IS CAPTIVATED BY HER BEACHSIDE WEEKENDER. ITS WARM AND SUNNY LOCATION ON THE CENTRAL COAST, NORTH OF SYDNEY, SUITS THE PERSONALITY OF ONE OF AUSTRALIA'S MOST WELL-KNOWN MEDIA PRESENTERS AND THE SPOKESPERSON FOR A RANGE OF ICONIC AUSTRALIAN BRANDS. 'I HAVE A NICE HOUSE IN TOWN, BUT THIS MEANS I CAN TAKE FRIENDS AWAY AND SPEND QUALITY TIME WITH THEM, SHARING A FEW QUIET MEALS AND WALKING ON THE BEACH,' SHE SAYS. THE 1940s SPANISH-MISSION-STYLE BUNGALOW IS A STONE'S THROW FROM

Far left, the dining room where guests eat breakfast when it's too cool to be outside; **centre**, Deborah relaxing with a cup of coffee; **this page**, the living area is for people to 'flop on the couch and put their feet on the table'.

DEBORAH HUTTON

Right, Deborah in her kitchen. On the shelves are botanical prints by Tara Kain and Meghan McGann; **below**, collections of shells are displayed throughout the house; **opposite page**, French timber candlesticks in a corner of the living room; the lamp is made from an urn Deborah picked up in Mittagong and a shade her mother had made at Bloomingdale's.

the beach. Its three bedrooms and bunkhouse provide ample room for sleep-over guests, while the bright, airy open-plan living area spills onto a glorious shaded deck. On cooler days guests can eat in the dining room at a large timber table that came with the house. In short, it is the perfect spot for all manner of relaxation and indulgence.

A gregarious host, Deborah loves indulging her close-knit circle of family and friends with good food, good wine and a comfortable place to wind down. When it came to the interior, the design brief was simple – make people feel at home.

'This is a real entertaining house,' she says. 'The hub of the home is the kitchen and barbecue and, because the design is all open plan, people can just sit around and relax. I didn't want a house that felt untouchable. I want the people that come here to feel they can flop on the couch and put their feet on the table.'

Around the house are collections of shells, flowers and white French timber candlesticks all blended to create a homely atmosphere. She uses her own homewares range of linen and dinnerware when accommodating and catering for her guests.

Despite her intensive work commitments, Deborah is disciplined when it comes to the weekend. 'The phone is turned off when I come here. I don't want to know. It's the one thing I'm selfish about. I'll speak to you Friday afternoon, and then you won't hear from me until Monday morning.'

GIOVANNI D'ERCOLE JEWELLERY DESIGNER

MOTHER NATURE BECKONS FROM ALMOST EVERY ROOM OF GIOVANNI D'ERCOLE'S BYRON BAY ABODE. AND SURPRISINGLY, FOR A MAN WHO'S MADE HIS FORTUNE FROM ORNATE, GOTHIC-STYLE JEWELLERY, THERE'S NOT A VELVET CURTAIN OR DARK WOODEN ARCH IN SIGHT. INSTEAD, HIS ONE-BEDROOM HILL-TOP CONSTRUCTION WITH ITS OPEN-PLAN DESIGN EMBRACES SIMPLICITY AND THE BREATHTAKING VIEWS THAT SURROUND IT. THIS STUNNING LOCATION, SAYS GIOVANNI, OWNER OF LOVE & HATRED IN SYDNEY'S STRAND ARCADE, IS THE KEY TO HIS CREATIVITY.

Far left, timber walls and sliding doors give the house its open look, the kitchen has a bush view; **centre**, Giovanni; **this page**, a makeshift chaise covered in Indian fabric beckons invitingly on the south-facing deck.

GIOVANNI D'ERCOLE

Right, instead of tiles the bathroom is a mix of stone, wood, Indonesian green stone and pebbles; **below**, wood and coconut heads found in a second-hand store; **opposite page**, lying on his French bed, Giovanni can keep track of the surf just outside his fron door. The bedside table is Moroccan.

A change of pace was behind Giovanni's decision to move from Sydney to Byron Bay. In keeping with his new calmer life, he took his time planning his beach retreat. He lived there for a year before he rebuilt and then another year before he began decorating. 'At first I lived with the bare minimum – a television and a mattress on the floor – simply because I preferred to live with nothing and then gradually fill my house with special pieces. I pretty much have an idea of what I'm looking for, and as I'm cruising around it eventually comes to me and I buy it.'

He also kept an eye on where the sun shone and how the wind blew through the block in order to complete what he calls the 'first stage' of his home (there are more rooms planned for under the house).The result is a mixed masterpiece that not only borrows from Mother Nature, but imitates her via materials like the bamboo-lining on the ceiling coated with green lacquer. 'I liked the idea of the house opening up so you're actually living with the elements,' he explains. 'When there's a lightning storm you're right amongst it, and when it's a balmy day it catches the slightest breeze. It's important to have that airiness and light.'

Giovanni has decorated his home with a blend of materials and pieces bought from near and far. From the European timber walls to Indian fabrics on the chaise and island-style coconut heads on the wall, there are countless eye-catching features. Yet this proliferation of cultures and styles hasn't cluttered the home at all. The house has an atmosphere of calm, facilitated by everything from the mood lighting to slide-away doors. 'Even the runners in the drawers are really quiet,' he says. 'There are no harsh noises in my house.'

Left, ornate original features frame the hallway; **below**, the couple on their deck; **opposite page**, bookcases dominate the living room; the table was bought at an antique store's closing sale. On the mantelpiece a letter 'E' from Paris sits next to an antique cheese board.

LISA WILKINSON EDITOR AND PETER FITZSIMONS AUTHOR AND JOURNALIST

'I REALLY LOVE MY HOME, AND I THINK A HOUSE SAYS A LOT ABOUT THE PERSONALITY OF THE PEOPLE WHO LIVE THERE,' SAYS MAGAZINE EDITOR LISA WILKINSON, WHO IS NOT A FAN OF MINIMALISM. 'I DON'T KNOW HOW PEOPLE LIVE IN HOUSES WITH WHITE WALLS, ONE COUCH AND ONE TABLE WITH AN APPLE SITTING IN THE MIDDLE OF IT.' LISA AND HER HUSBAND, AUTHOR AND JOURNALIST PETER FITZSIMONS, LIVE WITH THEIR THREE

E
H. Waldner

LISA WILKINSON AND PETER FITZSIMONS

Top, left to right, a French period chair that Lisa fell in love with stands in front of the window seat; the painting by Adrian Lockhart was a wedding present from Peter's family; vintage finds are scattered through the house. **Bottom, right to left**, Louis having breakfast in the kitchen; the bathroom still has an original 1903 toilet, which was re-enamelled; Lisa's study provides another chance to put the colour red on display.

children and their dog in an enchanting two-storey Edwardian house on Sydney's lower North Shore.

She is a keen collector of vintage wares and antiques. In the six years, the family has lived there she has filled the heritage-listed residence with treasures picked up locally and during holidays to France, where she is willingly drawn to flea markets.

'I love Clignancourt market in Paris,' she says. 'It's about the size of the city of Sydney, and like an open-air antique store where you can pick up amazing bargains. I still get pleasure from the things I've bought in France. I love that you see a five-dollar painting next to an expensive mirror, and in many ways the eye is drawn more to the painting.'

A self-confessed hunter-gatherer with a penchant for 19th-century portraits, 16th-century armoires and objects that tell a story, Lisa's assembly of period pieces has created a delightful retreat, at once sophisticated and playful, which provides constant visual stimulation and pleasure. Yet while the interiors are undeniably striking to look at, the overall ambience is decidedly cosy, comfortable and very family friendly.

'I have a thing for red. For me, it's the best decorating trick ever – it goes with everything. Red is a colour your eye is always drawn to, and it's really welcoming. I love a house you can walk into and feel instantly at home. I love fresh flowers, lots of books, dogs and kids, and the feeling that people don't have to mind the furniture.'

BATHING
CAPS

BATHING
CAPS
5/6

DAVID BROMLEY ARTIST
AND TORI DIXON-WHITTLE ACTOR AND MODEL

'I'D SAY IT WAS THE RESULT OF ONE MAN, MANY BOTTLES OF HOME-MADE WINE AND A CONCRETE MIXER,' SAYS ARTIST DAVID BROMLEY, LAUGHING, AS HE DESCRIBES THE ORIGINAL CONDITION OF THREE ADELAIDE BUILDINGS – A PAIR OF BLUESTONE GEORGIAN-STYLE COTTAGES AND A COACH HOUSE – THAT HE AND PARTNER TORI HAVE TURNED INTO A VIBRANT INNER-CITY HOME. PART OF THE PROPERTY DATES BACK TO THE

Far left, the outdoor eating area has a display niche featuring an old wooden Indian club and painted skittles; **centre**, David, Tori and Opey; **this page**, the front room. David's painting *Blue Boy* hangs over a Japanese timber packing box. The chairs are mid-century Danish design, the blue door was found discarded at the back of the property.

Right, an early painting of David's titled *Topsy Turvy* hangs in the dining room, the banquette chairs were covered in canvas; **below**, on the dining table is a Danish bowl filled with handpainted antique ceramic balls. The material is African Kuba cloth; **opposite page**, the guest bedroom features one of David's nudes, *Romy*. On the shelf above are hand-carved printing blocks from India and an old timber cutlery box.

1806s and the cottages have had a chequered past. After their original service in the 1860s as loading rooms for Cobb and Co stables staff, they'd been turned into a boarding house during the 1930s or '40s. The Greek-born owner had knocked the two cottages together, joining them to the coach house behind and rendering nearly every wall with thick concrete.

The buildings suffered during their years as a boarding house, falling further and further into disrepair, until eventually becoming a squat. By the time David and Tori bought them, only a few stray cats lived there. Rooms had been divided using cheap wood-grain panelling and sheets of taped-up plastic. The corrugated-iron roof had just about rusted through.

'But the configuration of the original buildings was beautiful,' says David. 'To take away from that would have destroyed the whole character. Our job was to clean, strengthen and simplify by paring back the makeshift additions. The character of the three buildings was pretty constant, but where it wasn't, we pulled it together with render and paint. And that's what's made it more organic.'

'We've put 2000 kilograms of render into the place and 500 litres of paint,' says Tori. 'White paint,' adds David, 'in keeping with the Greek heritage. But the interior aesthetic isn't simply Mediterranean, but artistically rustic. Between them, David and Tori have a wonderful collection of old Australian farmhouse furniture, as well as objects from all over the world that Tori imports for a small business she has. With so many rooms, many don't have a strict purpose other than as exhibition spaces for the collection. And, of course, the walls throughout are hung with paintings, most created by David but a few by fellow contemporary Australian artists.

DAVID BROMLEY AND TORI DIXON-WHITTLE

Right, seagrass matting covers the floor of the living room; an old timber bench serves as a bookshelf; the painting is by Keren Seelander, the pitchforks came from Spain; **below**, in the bedroom an antique bedspread from India makes an elaborate contrast to the austere Australian stoneware bottles displayed on the shelf; the box on top of the chest of drawers was once used to hold kimono; **opposite page**, on the wall of the master bedroom, an abstract mural, copied from a textile design found in a magazine, was painted onto the wall.

Apart from a brightly patterned orange Indian bedcover thrown across the master bed, the larger pieces of furniture, such as sofas and armchairs, are clad in white canvas covers that reduce their impact in the rooms. This leaves the artwork and objects to be the heroes, and plays up the texture of the hand-hewn, roughly rendered walls and the natural floor-coverings.

'We approached reworking the place in a hearty way,' says David. 'The walls are thick and roughly rendered, inside and out, so we needed a gutsy approach. If we'd put in domestic-scale materials, they would have been overshadowed by the building.'

The floors in the two front entrance rooms are covered in thick, rectangular sheets of lime-washed plywood, their edges bevelled to resemble tiles. As you move further into the heart of the house (the living and dining rooms), the plywood makes way for nubbly seagrass matting. In the hallway and kitchen at the rear, the floor surface changes again, this time to smooth concrete pavers that continue outside into a partially covered courtyard.

A flight of steps painted a deep Aegean Sea blue leads upstairs to the first floor of the coach house: the master bedroom, dressing room and ensuite. A doorway from the bathroom leads onto a north-facing rooftop deck – both it and the bathroom floor are also painted in the same deep blue, custom-mixed colour.

'To some people, our approach would not be seen as all that pragmatic,' says David. 'But this is how we like to live. Our work has been the dominant part of our lives for so long that the house will now play an important role in defining our residential life. It's a very private space – a real retreat.'

Left, a Snelling chair sits in front of an unpainted wall in Pam's warehouse home; **below**, Pam and Lydia; **opposite page**, the living area in Pam's house features a formal dining table and mismatched chairs.

PAM EASTON AND LYDIA PEARSON FASHION DESIGNERS

'I COULDN'T IMAGINE GOING OUT AND BUYING A WHOLE LOT OF NEW FURNITURE AND THEN STYLING IT IN A CERTAIN WAY. TO ME THAT DOESN'T EXPRESS YOUR PERSONALITY OR CHARACTER,' SAYS PAM EASTON, PART-OWNER OF THE EASTON PEARSON FASHION AND HOMEWARES LABEL. PAM LIVES ONLY THREE DOORS UP FROM THE RETAIL BUSINESS SHE CREATED WITH LYDIA PEARSON. AND YET THE WAREHOUSE APARTMENT SHE SHARES WITH ARCHITECT HUSBAND ROBERT RIDDEL AND THEIR DAUGHTER NINA HAS ITS OWN QUIRKY AND DISTINCT TOUCH.

Right, Pam has brought the garden indoors with a collection of plants and French wrought-iron chairs; **below,** the kitchen sideboard displays some of Pam's collection of glassware and cups; **opposite page**, a favourite ceramic vase sits on top of a late 19th-century sideboard. The artwork is by Luke Roberts, the sculpture cast came from the old Queensland College of Art.

When Pam first saw the old, four-storey Goldenia Tea building, her first thought was that it would be a great place to live. 'It's in the CBD and yet it has views of the Brisbane River and a small park, as well as a three-street frontage. The long views make it feel like there's lots of space around it. We're also within walking distance of the main shopping areas and Brisbane city. All these things make it a very nice place to be,' she says.

Inside, Robert has divided the space into inviting areas that catch the sun, making them special places to spend time at the weekends. A large kitchen opens to an informal living area, a space to flop into big chairs covered with Rajasthani throws. Each morning, the family can be found in the light-filled breakfast room. There Pam also tends to her 'indoor garden', which is full of herbs and orchids, and even has a lemon tree.

Through the winter, a combined living and dining room provides a large space for entertaining friends, while in summer they dine at night by the glow of the city on the enormous rooftop terrace.

Downstairs in the Easton Pearson shop, Pam and Lydia's shared sense of aesthetics is displayed in the collection of accessories, collectables, and the traditional cloth fabrics comprising their EP Manchester range. 'We can easily go into a shop full of 5000 things and pick out the same item,' says Lydia, 'and yet our lives are really quite different.'

LYDIA PEARSON

Right, Lydia on the steps of the Victorian timber house she shares with her family; **below**, in the hallway is a painting by Michael Barnett showing Lydia's husband Robin's first restaurant; **opposite page**, the living room. A much-loved couch is covered in Indian fabric cushions.

Preferring to distance herself from work, Lydia, the other half of the fashion label, and her family live in a beautiful Victorian timber house in the suburbs. It's where she, husband Robin Ilett, and their three children often enjoy weekend dinners with large groups of family and friends.

Robin and Lydia had admired the flaking facade of the house for many years before they bought it. They had outgrown two nearby cottages and were looking for a free-flowing home.

The interior of Lydia's house reflects this casual family warmth, but she won't be pinned down on describing the style as any in particular. 'Oh, believe me, it's just happened. I didn't want something that looked ethnic or European, but something that was a pastiche of different feelings and styles, so it couldn't be put in a box.' Most importantly though, it's about comfort.

The spacious living room, kitchen and back garden are usually where the family hang out or play host to their many visitors. 'We always have our Saturday breakfast in the kitchen,' she says. 'It's the only morning the whole family can get together. We grab the newspapers and sit around listening to *The Comfort Zone* on Radio National and reading horoscopes.'

In the living room huge windows overlooking the front verandah bring the mood of the day's weather inside. A much-loved living room couch and an assortment of chairs are covered with brightly coloured Indian cushions, which, Lydia jokes, cover up the holes in the fabric. With its yellow-painted timber walls the room has a cheery feel. Floor-to-ceiling shelves are stacked with books, wines and games.

Lydia's own creations adorn walls and ceilings. She created a wall-

Right, Lydia made the wall hanging from a friend's unfinished painting, an Indian miniature and a length of Javanese embroidery; **below**, the hallway has tent-stripes painted along it, which are carried through to the ceiling in the bedroom; **opposite page**, Lydia and Robin created a 'chandelier' out of a collection of old lamp fittings.

hanging by combining a friend's unfinished painting, Indian miniatures and a length of Javanese embroidered felt, and in the bedroom a collection of old lamp-fittings hang in a group. Lydia and Robin had wanted to buy a chandelier, but they couldn't find one that 'looked sensible' so they made their own version.

When she needs time to herself, Lydia escapes to her bedroom. 'It's the only place I might find time for myself on the weekend,' she says. 'The striped ceiling was inspired by Empire-style tents. I love the feeling that I'm under a canopy.' The stripes idea spills out into the walls of the hallway which she adorns with collections of flowers or leaves from a friend's garden or from her own. Like everything else in the house, the floral arrangements have a charmingly haphazard air.

The informality extends to the style of living. When the couple entertain, nothing is overly structured. The house and the back garden are the scene of large relaxed dinners which dissolve into nights of games and cards. Robin and Lydia prepare the food together; she shuns entrees and mains in favour of four or five dishes, usually French or Vietnamese in origin (among other things, she and Pam share a passion for Asian food). Sometimes the children have their dinner in one room, the adults in another.

CHARLIE BROWN FASHION DESIGNER

WEEKENDS ARE VERY BLACK AND WHITE FOR DESIGNER CHARLIE BROWN. THE DISTINCTIVE TWO-TONE COLOUR SCHEME OF HER VILLA AT THE SHERATON MIRAGE GOLD COAST RESORT IN QUEENSLAND IS A REFLECTION OF HER SEXY URBAN-CHIC STYLE. 'WHY IS THE VILLA ALL IN BLACK AND WHITE? IT'S A BIT LIKE MY CHARACTER, WOULDN'T YOU SAY?' SHE SAYS. EVEN THOUGH THE MAIN BEACH VILLA SOMETIMES DOUBLES AS A SHOWROOM, IT'S MOSTLY USED AS A WEEKEND RETREAT FOR CHARLIE AND HER FAMILY: HUSBAND DANNY AVIDAN, THEIR TWO CHILDREN, DAVID AND FRANCESCA,

Far left, the three-seater couch is covered in charcoal fabric; **centre**, Charlie in her living room; **this page**, the white dining room. The highly decorative mirror was bought in Bali.

Right and opposite page, the custom-made table in the bedroom was a gift to Danny from Charlie; **below**, David and Francesca in their white bedroom.

and Charlie's daughter Sophie (when she's back in Australia on holidays).

'I don't want to fuss while I'm here,' Charlie admits. 'I want time to relax with my family, so the villa's interior was designed to be ultra low-maintenance.' Architect Iain Halliday consulted on the minimal renovations while Charlie added her designer touch to the finer details.

The starkness of the colour scheme is broken up by the use of fabrics with different textures and patterns, a mix of decorative and simple furnishings, large mirrors and changing colour features – white floors, black walls; black floors, white walls.

There's the simple round black dining-room table and the leather-upholstered white dining chairs; the white custom-made table set against the black feature wall in the bedroom; and in the children's bedroom, black-and-white photographs add life and colour to an otherwise white colour scheme.

In the living room a large hexagonal window above the charcoal sofa could be taken for a photograph. The green bamboo stems seen outside appear to be arranged for artistic display.

'Compared to my usual passion for beautiful things, this place is sparse and functional,' says Charlie. 'It's all about freeing ourselves from the clutter of life and having the time to hang out together as a family.' When they are not enjoying the beach or pool, this usually involves zipping around to the local shops and restaurants in their reconditioned VW Beetle – a black and white affair in keeping with the style of the weekend.

Left, bromeliads which need little care sit in rough stone pots outside David Adams's front door; **below**, the film-maker; **opposite page**, in the hallway wooden columns from Rajasthan frame the mud walls. The chandelier is from Morocco, the screen-prints are of Balinese royalty.

DAVID ADAMS DOCUMENTARY FILM-MAKER

'THE ORGANIC NATURE OF STONE, MUD AND ROUGH WOOD CREATES A SPIRIT AND AN AMBIENCE THAT'S NOT POSSIBLE WITH OTHER MATERIALS,' SAYS DOCUMENTARY FILM-MAKER AND PHOTOJOURNALIST DAVID ADAMS. 'YOU INSTINCTIVELY WANT TO RUN YOUR HANDS ACROSS THE EARTHY WALLS AND WALK BAREFOOT ACROSS THE FLOORBOARDS.' DAVID, WHO IS RESPONSIBLE FOR THE ACCLAIMED *JOURNEYS TO THE ENDS OF THE EARTH* SERIES, HAS ALWAYS BEEN DRAWN TO ADOBE ARCHITECTURE. HIS HOUSE ON SYDNEY'S NORTHERN BEACHES WAS DESIGNED BY ARCHITECT AND BUILDER

Right, the covered verandah. The hanging daybed is from India, the 1920s woven reed mat from the Trobriand islands in Papua New Guinea. Built-in shelves contain other finds including a cast-iron Chinese Buddha; **below,** the bathroom. David found the old rectory leadlight window in Goa, India. The indigo and turquoise floor and bath surround tiles are Moroccan; **opposite page,** the living room features a daybed from Bali and a low 'plank' table found in India.

Andrew Minter, renowned for his organic sensibility and mud-house designs.

Andrew's inspiration is Egyptian architect Hassan Fathy (1900–89), and he builds with a simple yet durable technique. Instead of the traditional straw and mud bricks, he uses tin over Hebel blocks or a wooden framework, before rendering it in layers of thick, coloured earth and sculpting it into gentle, undulating, curving lines.

Once the front doors of the house have heaved open, the power of the place hits you. The light streaks through exquisite 500-year-old hand-carved Mughal Indian stone screens known as jaalis, and a metal Moroccan chandelier casts luminous colour around the room. Three vivid red screen-prints compel you to head across the kauri pine wood floor, which was recycled from an old church at Penrith in western Sydney. From there, you head down the stairs, past wooden columns from Rajasthan and through the first light-filled pavilion, walking by the guest bedrooms and library.

'I really wanted to build a home that took friends on a journey to faraway places, to a different time and space, and away from their worries to enjoy the moment we were sharing,' says David. His passion for exploration – inspired by his late father – extends from skiing the sand dunes of Africa's Ténéré desert to being the last person to photograph the ancient statues of Buddha in Bamiyan, Afghanistan, before they were destroyed by the Taliban, so it's no wonder he has brought home a pure, romantic, creative energy.

David's house is a sensory experience full of the energy and richness of other worlds. 'It has been built with the heart – all the time feeling that I was building a true home, the one place I would want to happen upon if I was travelling.'

SIECLE

Left, the outside of Carole Muller's 1890s timber-clad boatshed home; **below**, Carole in the library; **opposite page**, the antique chair is upholstered in 17th-century Verdure tapestry fabric. On the wall above it is one of a pair of neo-classical papier mache figures which once hung in a theatre in Paris.

CAROLE MULLER ARTIST

WHEN ARTIST CAROLE MULLER FOUND AN OLD BOATSHED PERCHED RIGHT ON THE EDGE OF LAVENDER BAY, WITH A BREATHTAKING VIEW OF THE OPERA HOUSE AND HARBOUR BRIDGE, SHE DISCOVERED A SYDNEY-LOVER'S PARADISE. SHE WAS SO SMITTEN WITH THE CHARACTER-FILLED TIMBER BUILDING, WHICH HAD SEVERAL APARTMENTS ON ITS FIRST FLOOR AND BOAT-CHARTER PREMISES BELOW, SHE BOUGHT IT ON THE SPOT. 'IT WAS SO ROMANTIC, I COULDN'T RESIST,' SHE SAYS. 'I MEAN, A BOATSHED RIGHT ON THE EDGE OF SYDNEY HARBOUR – AND WITH SUCH A VIEW! PLUS, IT'S CLOSE

CAROLE MULLER

Right, the living area has had the false ceiling removed to expose the rafters. Carole painted the hoop pine floorboards with a light grey liming paint to make the room look lighter. The furniture is a mix of antique styles collected from around the world.

to everything – I can get the ferry to Circular Quay, and I can walk to Kirribilli.'

The boatshed was built in the 1890s and had been reclad and reroofed in the 1970s, over the top of the original cladding materials. The end apartment, in which Carole now resides, had originally been a sail-maker's loft, and former owners had turned it into a rabbit warren of dark rooms.

'We gutted the interior to get back to the bones,' she says. 'I used the structure of the building as a guide for renovating. But I didn't realise just how wonderful it was going to be when I started.'

With the help of a structural engineer and a builder, Carole redesigned the space, creating a shorter central corridor with a bedroom on either side. The front door now leads into a book-lined library. There was enough space behind the master bedroom to turn the second bathroom into an ensuite, allowing the front half of the apartment to be devoted to one open-plan living, dining and kitchen area, all facing the spectacular view.

'My aim was to create a big sense of space,' she says. Painted white, a row of windows punctuates the ceiling's northern side, allowing sunlight to penetrate the living area, while another two, on the southern side, frame views of the Bridge and the Opera House.

Her love of antiques and Asian artefacts – as well as her continuing connection to Bali, where she has a home as well – is obvious throughout her home. The pristine walls form the perfect backdrop for her elegant pieces, many acquired for her last home, the neo-Gothic Bronte House.

Although she sighs when she says she misses swimming at Bronte beach, Carole concedes that her harbourside boatshed more than makes up for it.

SASKIA HAVEKES FLORIST

STEPS DESCENDING PAST BOUGAINVILLEA, ELEPHANT PALMS AND MAGNOLIA, AS WELL AS RARITIES SUCH AS A MADAGASCAN SUEDE PLANT, TRANSPORT YOU TO TROPICAL CLIMES AND THE HOME OF SYDNEY FLORIST SASKIA HAVEKES. 'WE FELT LIKE WE'D LIVED HERE FOR AGES WHEN WE FIRST MOVED IN,' SAYS SASKIA. 'IT HAS SUCH A LOVELY AMBIENCE.' THE HOUSE IN WOOLLAHRA WAS BUILT IN THE 1920s AND NESTLES ALMOST OUT OF SIGHT FROM STREET LEVEL. SASKIA'S PARTNER, PHOTOGRAPHER GARY HEERY, CALLS THEIR HOME 'SLEEPY HOLLOW', A REFERENCE TO ITS

Far left, a tranquil outdoor space; **centre**, Saskia with some of her favourite things; **this page**, the photograph of a rose is by Saskia's partner, Gary Heery. The wooden table was her mother's.

Right, a Moroccan lamp hangs over the revamped staircase; **below**, another of Gary's photos of a 'Queen of the Night' tulip; **opposite page**, Gary bought the 1890s table at an antique store.

site on the edge of an escarpment and the local bird and animal life. 'It's possum central,' he says. From the back, views through trees and over rooftops look down to the blue of Double Bay.

'It's usually a full-tilt windmill in here,' says Saskia, sitting in the area off the kitchen that is the hub of family life. They share their home with their two daughters, Ginger and Sunday, and Gary's daughter Ruby.

The pretty three-bedroom house is full of interesting nooks. Saskia fell in love with the first-floor addition – once an artist's studio – which now contains the main bedroom and a sitting room. 'It's a really peaceful place,' she says. 'That was the thing I loved. And the vista outside – all those trees. Up here it's my tree house. There's a lot of bird life. One night an owl flew right into the kitchen.'

Another appealing feature was the layout, which recalled the house in Kenthurst, Sydney, where Saskia lived as a child. 'We had no doors inside except for the bathroom. It was all open plan and, in its day, very unusual.'

Downstairs are two small bedrooms, a bathroom and two living areas. One leads on to the front garden, lending itself to alfresco dining; the other, nearer the kitchen, adjoins a verandah with views down to the bay. An old wooden swing seat invites you to linger.

Gary and Saskia plan to extend the verandah, enlarge the kitchen, maybe add another bedroom – but so far have contented themselves with renovating the existing structure. 'We pulled up hectares of old, worn carpet and every room was in a different colour paint – all enamel! The woodwork was dark, so the overall effect was very heavy. And every window was nailed shut and covered with security roller blinds,' Saskia says.

Right, the sofa in the upstairs studio-turned-living room is decorated with cushions picked up from a market and an embroidered Indian wedding shawl draped over the back; **below**, the light, bright bedroom; **opposite page**, the dark wood of a Jacobean table setting offsets the vibrant blue of Gary's favourite chair.

They removed a 'terrible outdoor railing' on the indoor stairs, stripped back the paint, coated the walls in white and stained the floor with Japan black. 'The floor people were nervous about putting the black on,' says Saskia. 'They thought we were mad and tried to convince us to keep the floors light.'

The couple's vision paid off, however, and the house is now a light, open showcase for the treasures they've collected over the years. Saskia loves trawling markets and old furniture shops. 'My dad did that, too,' she says. 'We used to go to Paddy's Markets every Saturday morning. With the shop, I am out sourcing things all the time.' Finds include an old wooden table (circa 1890) that was originally used on Cockatoo Island, a spectacular Indian wedding shawl that now graces the back of a sofa, and a pair of beautiful gold and turquoise Moroccan pouffes.

Meanwhile, the garden is blooming. 'We've done a lot of work there,' says Saskia. 'We put in a stone wall and a lot of metalwork. We've redone the steps as they were narrow and dangerous. And there's a lot of new planting. We're even trying to get a hedge going.

'I buy the plants and say where I think they should go, but Gary does most of the planting and reshuffling. There's a big patch of flowering ginger that smells beautiful, and all the strelitzias are amazing when they flower.'

Saskia admits she is reluctant to pick flowers from her own garden. 'I see so many cut flowers, it's nice to see something actually growing.' Instead Gary's dramatic floral photography, potted plants and vases of fresh colourful flowers from her business fill every room of the house with the natural beauty they both thrive on.

Left, two yellow sofas from Natalie's former house now sit happily in her second living room; **below**, Natalie Bloom; **opposite page**, the light-filled main living room features a swinging Bubble chair by Finnish designer Eero Aarnio. The Arco lamp is by Italian designer Achille Castiglione.

NATALIE BLOOM FOUNDER OF BLOOM COSMETICS

AS YOU STEP THROUGH THE IMPOSING DARK WOOD DOORS, YOU SUDDENLY FEEL VERY SMALL UNDER THE SOARING CEILINGS AND ABUNDANCE OF LIGHT. A HOME THAT EXUDES SUCH SERENITY WHEN YOU ARRIVE BELIES THE FRANTIC SCHEDULE OF ITS OWNERS: NATALIE BLOOM, CREATOR OF THE BLOOM COSMETICS EMPIRE, AND HER HUSBAND BRIAN HAMERSFELD. SITUATED IN A LEAFY CENTRAL SUBURB NEAR MELBOURNE'S YARRA RIVER, THEIR HOME IS A WELCOMING BASE BETWEEN BUSINESS AND RETAIL EXCURSIONS IN MELBOURNE AND AROUND THE WORLD.

NATALIE BLOOM

Right, Natalie fell in love with this painting by Matthew Johnson which hangs in the living room; **below**, the bathroom makes a serene contrast to the vibrant colours in the rest of the house; **opposite page**, the cocktail lounge. The shaggy wool rug and chocolate sofas were custom-made, the lacquered MDF screen was designed by interior designer Kerry Phelan.

The rooms too are overwhelming – a happy collision between a grand old Melbourne home and a cool inner-city apartment. A slick, state-of-the-art kitchen and dining room snuggle up next to a small second living room where family portraits, paintings by Melbourne artist Mirka Mora and the couple's black and white wedding photographs adorn the walls.

The international success of Bloom propels Natalie around the world every year, and she often picks up pieces for the house. 'It allows me to bring back really interesting things. I love Paris and the Nolita district in New York. But honestly, I do think you can get everything you want right here. Australian style is so eclectic.' One of her favourite purchases is a huge purple and mauve painting by Melbourne-based artist Matthew Johnson, which hangs in the main living room.

At nearby Chapel Street, Natalie often picks up kitsch bits and pieces as well as vintage toys for Brian's collection. There's also a local nursery for sourcing fragrant plants for her expanding garden. The original garden was one of the main reasons they bought the house, but it suffered during the renovations, and all they were able to keep were two huge eucalypts. 'There's space for a garden around the entire house so we're creating a very lush, overgrown, Edna Walling-style garden with plants that are either edible, add colour and scent, or indicate a change in season.'

Apart from having family around, Natalie and Brian's weekends are a whirl of parties, dinners or drinks at home. The designated party room is located off the main living room and is a modernist cocktail lounge with circular mirrors hung on a bright orange wall, floor-to-ceiling drapes and chocolate suede sofas.

KEN DONE ARTIST

'I'M A CANCERIAN AND I HAVE TO BE NEAR THE WATER ALWAYS,' EXPLAINS ARTIST KEN DONE. 'MOST WEEKENDS, MY WIFE JUDY WILL SPEND TIME IN THE GARDEN – THAT'S VERY MUCH HER DOMAIN. I TEND TO DRIFT INTO THE SEA.' HIS ESTATE AT CHINAMAN'S BEACH IN SYDNEY'S MIDDLE HARBOUR CONTAINS THREE HOUSES, BUT THE ONE HE IS MOST SENTIMENTAL ABOUT IS 'THE CABIN', A PLACE HE FIRST SAW WHEN HE WAS 14 (THE YEAR HE STARTED AT THE NATIONAL ART SCHOOL IN EAST SYDNEY), AND WOULD SIT ON THE ROCKS AT THE END OF THE

Far left, 'The Cabin' where Ken often spends his weekends is a cute, rugged space where even the rock walls have been left untouched; **centre**, Ken with one of his paintings; **this page**, a glimpse through the wooden doors of the living area to Ken's smallest studio, his favourite place to paint on the weekends.

KEN DONE

Right, Ken in the kitchen of 'The Cabin' which overlooks his beloved harbour; **below**, a sunny corner of the living area; **opposite page**, the pinboard over Ken's work bench is crowded with pictures of family and friends.

beach, believing that he could will himself into ownership of it. 'I suppose it's silly to have such a passion for a space,' he says.

The white-walled cabin is anything but silly. It's a beautiful little studio/home built into rocks near the water's edge and exuding a holiday atmosphere – via the coat racks laden with sunhats and flippers – with a self-contained work space for its creative owner. Here is where Ken likes to spend most weekends and although it's his smallest studio (he also has one in Redfern and one in another house on the estate) the views surrounding it are expansive. The simple practical furnishings and stone (even rock) wall structures inside suggest it's a place for tuning into nature. The beach-coloured tones of reclining white-painted cane chairs, a cream rug and the light-coloured timber floors in the living room are soothing. Louvred windows in all the rooms allow the scent of the sea to waft throughout the place and reveal the abundance of natural bush outside.

Close by is his 'cave', complete with a gnome and another stupendous harbour view. 'A lot of Australian guys want to have a shed, but I always wanted to have a cave,' he says, and laughs. Ken often retires here after breakfast on a Sunday to paint or just relax and think. 'This is a separate block of land and I guess a lot of people would want to put a big house on it, but all we wanted was to have a beautiful garden and a cave,' he says. 'Here you can either simply be in the space, fish, or you can make drawings.'

And his favourite artworks? 'The very best pictures I own are drawings my kids did when they were little...their worth's beyond money.'

WHAT'S MY

MEGAN MORTON STYLIST

'AS A STYLIST, YOU SEE SO MUCH BEAUTIFUL STUFF YOUR EYES CAN GET SORE,' SAYS MEGAN MORTON. 'THIS HAS TAUGHT ME TO STEP BACK AND WAIT FOR THOSE BITS OF LOVE TO COME TO ME.' MEGAN, AND HER FAMILY – HUSBAND GILES AND CHILDREN MILLIE AND SEBASTIAN – REGULARLY ESCAPE THE HECTIC PACE OF SYDNEY AND UNWIND AT THEIR WEEKENDER IN BURRAWANG IN THE SOUTHERN HIGHLANDS. THEIR FOUR-BEDROOM HOME, CALLED 'THE BIG COUNTRY SLEEP', IS WHERE SHE CAN ENJOY A MORE INTUITIVE AND RELAXED APPROACH TO INTERIORS.

Far left, to bring more light into the dining room Megan Morton knocked out walls and added windows; **centre**, Megan with son Sebastian; **this page**, a smoky blue velvet chair in the living room sets off Megan's collection of bric-a-brac.

MEGAN MORTON

Right, the children's bedroom is an inviting mix of stripes, quilts and cubbyhole corners; **below**, Megan found the patchwork blankets on a trip to South Australia; **opposite page**, the canvas headboard in the main bedroom was painted by designer Tina de Salis.

The cottage-style home is all but hidden from the street by a 2.5-metre-high hedge arching over the gate. The front garden has a semi-formal parterre, planted with a box hedge, hellebore and maple trees, and a generous lawn is along the side. Once paved, the lawn now hosts croquet competitions and afternoon teas. 'I grew up on a banana farm, and I wanted to give Millie and Sebastian some of that feeling,' says Megan.

The interior style has hints of 'nanna' without being stuffy and old-fashioned; old-world meets new. 'I set myself a challenge to never spend more than $99 [on an item],' she says. Every weekend was spent scouring auction rooms, bric-a-brac stores and junk shops. One find, which admittedly blew her budget, was a sitting-room sofa and matching armchairs. Her family spent the previous year sitting on mattresses, but that didn't faze her.

This is not a monochrome household. 'I love colour,' says Megan, adding that choosing a soft palette and different themes for each room provides contrast to the white walls. Although the main bedroom is a dramatic mix of black and white, it remains warm and inviting. The painted headboard adds an informal refinement.

Her favourite room is Sebastian and Millie's bedroom. Originally every panel was a different heritage colour, but she opted for a powder blue. The room now has a lightness and whimsy that suits its function. 'I sometimes join the kids for an afternoon nap,' she says.

In Sydney Megan lives in a 'modern' way but she says, 'The beauty of a second house is that you are able to fill it with folly and have as many trinkets as you want.'

IAIN HALLIDAY INTERIOR DESIGNER

SITTING ON A LEDGE OF PERPENDICULAR ROCK, IAIN HALLIDAY'S HOME IS A RESTRAINED MULTI-LEVEL EYRIE. ORIGINALLY PLANNED AS A WEEKENDER, HIS HOUSE AT WHALE BEACH ON SYDNEY'S NORTHERN BEACHES HAS INSTEAD MORPHED INTO A GROOVY FULL-TIME PAD. THIS HOUSE IS A WAY OF ESCAPING,' SAYS IAIN, THE INTERIOR DESIGNER BEHIND MANY OF SYDNEY'S TRENDY INNER-CITY RESTAURANTS AND APARTMENTS. THE RETREAT, WHICH HE DESIGNED, IS HIS BASE FOR THE FEW HOURS A WEEK HE'S NOT AT THE COMPANY HE CO-DIRECTS, BURLEY KATON HALLIDAY (BKH),

Far left, a La Chaise chair designed by Charles Ray Eames is positioned to take in the best view; **centre**, Iain with Ace and Daphne; **this page**, the brilliant front door opens to reveal a mix of coral and a Warhol portrait of Chairman Mao.

IAIN HALLIDAY

Top row left to right, Iain at work, the photograph behind him is an untitled Bill Henson from the Paris Opera series; the hallway has light flooding in; the living room sofa is covered in Fortuny Palluco fabric. The stonefish are Indonesian. **Bottom row right to left**, the bathroom has a feature wall in Brunschwig and Fils wallpaper; Iain had the gate made after seeing the original one in a client's home; a Louis XVI chair is covered in striped Kenzo fabric.

the design firm with the winning minimalist streak. From the outside his home is almost modest, but the fun starts when you swing open the vibrantly coloured front door and come face-to-face with a pink-lipped Warhol print of Mao above a 19th century copy of a Louis XVI table – dressed with several pieces of coral. This is just one of many discreet 'galleries' where Iain displays favourite objects.

The witty decor is what Iain refers to as 'a collision of furniture'. This ability to mix styles with flair may come in part from his mother, Beth Halliday, who shares the beach house when she's in town and whose early career working with architects made a big impression on her young son. Iain went on to study interior design at Sydney College of the Arts and began a degree course in architecture. However, he dropped out and now has the distinction of being one of the country's most celebrated designers.

His work speaks for itself. The Whale Beach property was inspired by houses dotting the cliffs along Italy's Amalfi Coast, domiciles where Pucci playsuits, kitten heels and dry martinis are never out of place. 'I like the aesthetic of Italian interiors,' he says. 'Always hard floors – ceramic or stone tiles – and antiques mixed with slip-covered furniture.'

A particular favourite of his is the Rome apartment of American abstract painter Cy Twombly, which was commissioned in the 17th century for a member of the notorious Borgia clan. 'The apartment is very beautiful and very pale, with an enormous floor space and lots of old furniture strewn around,' he says. Iain's heady mix of antiques and clean, uncluttered lines echo is inspired by Twombly's place but his own capacity for interpreting 21st-century modern gives it a singular twist.

STEPHEN ORMANDY AND LOUISE OLSEN

What is so appealing about Louise Olsen and Stephen Ormandy's home is that it manages to defy strict classification. Yes, there are the designer furniture pieces – Eames, Bertoia, Paulin and Kjaerholm are all present and correct – and yes, there are the significant artworks. But mixed into this are inherited tables, locally sourced furniture, market finds, a whole host of objects picked up on their travels and their collection of colourful resin bowls, platters and vases from Dinosaur Designs. If I had to pick two words that sum up their style it would be 'colour' and 'relaxed'. There is a pleasing randomness (which is actually quite hard to achieve) that is the result of having an eye for colour, shape, proportion and a love of interesting objects.

Decorating tip A variety of objects displayed together works well if there is a loose colour theme. This allows a disparate selection of objects of different sizes and textures to work as a group.

TETSUYA WAKUDA

A picture of modern refinement, Tetsuya's home is the opposite of many of the other 'works in progress' featured here. He has chosen a restrained, masculine palette of materials, including wood, leather and chrome. His taste for matching Italian furniture creates a sense of luxury and sophistication, further enhanced by the placement of his favourite objects. Being a small collection, each item carries with it a great sense of significance.

The bold, textural artworks provide one of the most striking aspects of the decor. Their colour and energy are a perfect counterbalance to the controlled taste of the furnishings. For a man constantly on the move – working, travelling, fishing and socialising – one gets the sense that home is a refuge: a place that is calm, measured and beautiful.

Decorating tip A round table is often favoured by people who like to entertain, as it creates a communal feeling and encourages conversation to flow.

ADRIAN LEWIS

White is the dominating factor in Adrian's small one-bedroom apartment, the perfect backdrop for his collections of objects. While Adrian's taste is catholic, his decorating aesthetic is quite specific. What makes his apartment, and the many and varied things in it, work is the restricted palette. The whites here range from crisp and snowy through to soft creams. Against this are wood tones, gilt frames, mushroom velvet and honey-coloured coir matting. This tonal arrangement allows for an eclectic range of objects of a great historical and geographical diversity to blend seamlessly into the overall scheme.

Decorating tip In an apartment of such evident taste I was drawn to the way Adrian stacked books and magazines under a high white console. It gives them a sense of containment and their spines add a little hit of colour in an otherwise neutral space.

MARCIA HOSKING

There are some homes which exude earthiness and warmth, and this holiday house is one of them. It's marked by an uncompromising attitude to colour, from the red and yellow concrete tiles to the rich terracotta of the living room walls. Several key elements help build this successful style. The first is the choice of artworks, predominantly bold depictions of fruit and flowers and fecundity. Second is the choice of furnishings, in shades of eau de nil through to stronger greens. Third is the personalised collection of objects: the eccentric jugs stacked on top of punched-metal meat safes, the kitchen utensils stored in earthenware jars and the vintage suitcases stacked in the bedroom.

Decorating tip A colour that runs like a thread through the colour scheme of a house is a wonderfully unifying decorative device. It can be used in a major way on walls, or echoed in the furniture, soft furnishings, artworks or objects.

JULIE PATERSON

Julie Paterson's home signals a truly artistic spirit. The space itself is not what makes this apartment so interesting – it is *all* in the content. That said, it was the patina of the original plaster-work left exposed in her living room that has inspired many of her driftwood artworks. She admits to a liking for things left unfinished, be it in fabrics or interiors. Everywhere you look colourful artworks are layered, propped one on top of the other. There are two distinct palettes either strong and contrasting or soft and tonal and works tend to be grouped together according to their intensity. Artworks are assembled with a sense of symmetry. In other respects Julie has an immensely relaxed attitude to her home. She doesn't view her space as 'fixed' and as a result is always moving things around until they find a home.

Decorating tip Propping artworks as opposed to hanging them is a growing trend.

LEONA EDMISTON

At first glance there are few clues to the fact that this simple 1860s country cottage is the home of urban fashion designer Leona Edmiston and her husband Jeremy Ducker. The beauty of weekenders is that they are less uptight than their city counterpart because their purpose is enjoyment and relaxation. The set-up on Leona's verandah, a wonderfully inviting rattan sofa and striped cushions, is very telling of the life lived here. Comfort is a consideration inside; the built-in day bed with its pale upholstery and host of cushions creates a calm area to daydream or read. Would a detective pick-up on any clues as to the owner's profession? There is a give-away – the feather hats on the mantelpiece in the bedroom – not functional, not easy or comfortable, just impossibly glamorous.

Decorating tip Framing black and white prints with a generous surround of heavyweight cream card and a fine black frame gives a feeling of elegance to the simplest image.

JANE ROARTY

I first met Jane when she was a fashion editor working in London, and I couldn't help but be impressed by her immense personal style. When I moved to Sydney I saw how this translated into her home which is filled with the bold gestures of the truly confident: a vermilion wall dense with photographs, broad lemon stripes of paint in the guest bedroom, a chandelier in the kitchen and a fully dressed mannequin in the living room. Her all-time favourite look is the monochromatic schemes of Parisian designers in the 1930s. However, she acknowledges, 'the look was very expensive. My way out is to give my home a bohemian style. I can't afford minimalism.'

Decorating tip Jane has used a large piece of heavy, striped canvas as a curtain in the hallway close to the front door. It has the effect of introducing colour as you enter the house and the way that it is swept back with an ornate metal 'clasp' adds a sense of drama.

ZAHAVA ELENBERG

Often wonderful old buildings are carved up into areas no bigger than the average apartment and, due to a bit of exposed pipe work, are deemed 'warehouses' by over-zealous developers. Architect Zahava Elenberg's former textile-laminating factory is the real McCoy. A huge floor area, 250 square metres, has been turned into a living/working space for Zahava, her husband Callum Fraser and their daughter. As architects they have made conscious decisions about the building interior in terms of when to interfere and when to leave well alone, ensuring a degree of the original rawness was retained and even enhanced. This light-industrial shell is the context for Zahava and Callum's collection of exuberant contemporary art. Along with the bold furnishings, they give the space real verve and energy.

Decorating tip Don't buy art to match furniture – good art will always find its place.

DESIGN NOTES

GABRIELLE COURTENAY

At *Inside Out* we used the image of Gabrielle Courtenay's watermelon red bedroom as a cover image in April 2002. As her partner Gregory Smith points out, Gabrielle doesn't shy away from the full-strength option on the colour chart. She has hand-mixed many of the colours to get the exact tone she wants. As a counterbalance to the more moody shades, the walls in the living area are a vibrant avocado green which, as she points out, has the effect of bringing the outdoors in. She uses her own bold, floral artworks on her walls and creates stylish vignettes with generous bowls of flowers and wooden bowls, the deep coloured walls providing the perfect painterly backdrop.

Decorating tip When planning to paint, assemble all your colour samples (for all rooms) and look at them together. They should feel like a family in terms of tone. If you feel like being as bold as Gabrielle, try the same combination but three shades darker.

LYN GARDENER

Lyn Gardener has always had a flair for interior design, so when the opportunity came to showcase her latest decorating extravaganza *Inside Out* jumped at the chance. Here she has adopted a distinctly feminine approach. Lightness and brightness are the key to this look; five shades of white have been used to create a blank canvas on the walls, and the period mirrors, hung for decoration, also have the effect of bouncing light into the room from the nearby windows. Fabulous chandeliers sparkle by day and create interesting shadows by night. Into this context Lyn introduces a washed-out palette of pinks, champagne hues and light blues. Her home has a haphazard, bowerbird feeling, but the controlled palette and the consistent femininity mean it adheres to an overall scheme.

Decorating tip Lyn recommends that consistency is necessary to create this look. For example her crockery is mismatched but melds with a theme of faded colours, florals and plains that all work together.

DONALD CAMPBELL

There is a calm, gallery-like quality to Donald Campbell's structured and elegant city apartment which, when you see his art collection is entirely apt. Everything feels well considered, chosen and edited, be it a piece of furniture or one of his many artworks. Art plays an enormous role in this interior and the choices are a roll call of Australia's best artistic talent. Despite the seriousness of the art and the furniture, there is a real sense of warmth – provided by colour in the art and furnishings – and by the inclusion of decorating contrasts such as the 19th-century rug and the 18th-century tapestry in the bedroom. Witness the more relaxed side to Donald in his Northern Beaches holiday house where the decor is as simple as the pleasures.

Decorating tip Add a hint of mid-century style to your interior with the beautifully sculptural Yanagi 'Butterfly ' stool. Designed by Japanese Sori Yanagi in 1954 it is still in production and is available in rosewood and maple.

LEE MATHEWS

Those who love Lee Mathews's clothes are drawn by their enduring, timeless qualities – the offbeat fabrics, the hand-dyed colours and unpredictable touches that mark an independent spirit. Whether in her shops or at home she has a great intuitive sense of what works. She is fortunate to be married to a furniture maker who can take strange finds and make them beautiful. Their combined creative talents mean that their home is a happy collision of their respective input. Artworks are everywhere, dotted amongst the old business signs Guy bought at an auction. Add to this tin toys, cricket numbers and Lee's dresses. The house itself, with its fibro walls and wide balconies, enhances the sense of Australiana which Lee embraces.

Decorating tip Lee and Guy's home is about things they love but they also have the ability to have great big throwouts and start again. If you don't pay much for things, you have all the fun of redecorating.

STEPHEN JOLSON

Stephen Jolson has designed a space which functions beautifully. But then he has done something quite unexpected. He has decorated it with a mix of objects, art and furnishings that are actually quite difficult to make work together and has done it with ease. A 17th-century table, a couple of Cambodian rain drums, an original Corbusier lounge and some Moroccan lights make up his integrated and inspiring interior. How has he done it? The context is a good start. Basically, all the modern elements are soft, warm neutrals. The textural interest, the colour and the character are in the objects sourced during Stephen's travels – including the laser-cut screen, a copy of one he saw in India, which separates the master bedroom from the rest of the house. Contemporary ethnic has never looked so good.

Decorating tip All Stephen's photographs are shot on 35mm negative film as it can enlarged to A0 size before the dots begin to show.

LISA WILKINSON AND PETER FITZSIMONS

When Lisa Wilkinson enthuses about her home, she speaks of 'fresh flowers, books, dogs and kids'; for her it is about creating ambience and pleasure, about a context for family life with her children, her husband Peter FitzSimons, and, of course, Scout, the dog. The house itself is a grand, old Federation place with all its attributes intact. Into this space she has brought furniture that anchors the look in solidity and tradition. The skeleton of the look is fairly conservative. It is in the fleshing out that things get interesting. There is a love of disparate objects placed together with a sense of playfulness. Tradition has been combined with a quirky collector's eye for the interesting and off-beat, giving this rambling family home a sense of the unexpected.

Decorating tip Lisa feels that red is the hero of the decorating world, and she uses it liberally throughout her home's interior to give small hits of intensity.

DAVID BROMLEY AND TORI DIXON-WHITTLE

The restoration of David Bromley and his partner Tori Dixon Whittle's home was a labour of love, requiring copious amount of render and hundreds of litres of paint. The result, evocative of Greek buildings which are traditionally rendered and painted white, is, as David points out, gutsy, beautifully rough around the edges. 'Nothing is straight; everything is askew.' Into this space they have brought their collection of early Australian farmhouse furniture, some simple locally bought Danish chairs and a heap of art – both David's and that of his contemporaries. The combination of these elements produces a very textured, layered and interesting interior. One senses an artist's instinctive appreciation for how thing work together.

Decorating tip Strong punches of colour add energy to a simple interior. The concrete floor in David and Tori's all-white bathroom is painted a deep Aegean sea blue.

PAM EASTON LYDIA PEARSON

Pam Easton and Lydia Pearson's individuality as fashion designers is world class. And while the structures of their homes are very different, they hold in common a defined sense of what beauty is, and the importance of character and personality in a home. Pam has left her brick walls, distressed by time, untouched, which adds texture to her home along with a collection of mismatched chairs and local art.

Lydia's boldly striped ceiling of red and white is an inspiring decorative statement, simple yet effective. 'It just happened,' Lydia says of her house's style. But as often is the case with people who have innate taste, it has happened in a very appealing way.

Decorating tips Pam – when sourcing a setting of 'mismatching' dining chairs, try to ensure they are the same height and of similar wood. Lydia – her grouping of delicate glass light fittings makes a pretty central arrangement; make sure you hang them at varying lengths to create the right effect.

DESIGN NOTES

CHARLIE BROWN

There is no simpler interior design formula than that of black and white. While it may sound incredibly limiting, it actually opens up a host of decorating possibilities – and the beauty of it is that it is almost impossible to go wrong. Charlie Brown's sometime showroom/most time holiday villa is an example of a low-maintenance, functional space with all the high glamour attributes its owner requires. Within the stark palette there are moments of boldness (the stripes), moments of femininity (the chandeliers), and moments of opulence (the highly decorative mirrors). Decoratively each piece offsets another, always maintaining a balance between hard and soft, simple and elaborate, black and white.

Decorating tip If black and white is simply too stark for you, try introducing a third accent colour. Red and orange are strong and dramatic, but softer shades, such as beige and green, can also work well.

NATALIE BLOOM

Natalie Bloom's personal style provides clues to her leanings in decor. Even her choice of clothes spells out low-key luxury: functional, practical pieces with moments of flamboyance. And there in a nutshell is a description of her home. One of Australia's very best interior designers, Kerry Phelan, helped to orchestrate the major renovation of Natalie's 1912 home, and the result is muted elegance. But colour and pattern also have their place. The multi-coloured Matthew Johnson artwork, which Natalie fell in love with, the sunny yellow sofas and her ranunculi-covered ottoman all point to an exuberance and decorative energy amongst the tonal classics.

Decorating tip Colour and pattern add richness to an essentially neutral decorating palette. Try to keep the tones of uniform intensity and they will deliver a sense of surprise in different rooms of the house.

MEGAN MORTON

For years I had heard about stylist Megan Morton's country house in the Southern Highlands, and for years I had asked Megan when it would be ready to shoot. When 'The Big Country Sleep' (as the house is called) was eventually photographed, it lived up to everything one would imagine from a Megan Morton home. The period cottage has been subtly renovated to retain its charm but add a freshness and modernity. The result is airy, friendly and relaxed. Special groupings of objects have been sourced from various local auction rooms and junk shops and often have a pleasing tonal consistency. But the interior is not entirely an exercise in junk-shop chic. A counterbalance achieved by the bright white painted tongue-and-groove panelling, the rich polished floorboards and the smart zinc bench tops in the kitchen give this country cottage its twist.

Decorating tip Megan has used classic linen tea towels as material to cover the cushions of her dining chairs.

IAIN HALLIDAY

Interior decor, like fashion, is subject to the swing of the style pendulum – this year's maximalism can be last year's minimalism. Iain Halliday has always been ahead of the game; he has left minimalism behind and embraced a very modern eclecticism which only the design literate could pull off. Unusual juxtapositions characterise his home; a 1927 theatre lamp by Fortuny Palluco with a Louis XVI chair in a candy-stripe fabric by Kenzo; a modern freestanding bath beside a decorative feature wall of Brunschwig & Fils paper. Throw in some great art like Bill Henson's dramatic photographs and witness Halliday's sensibility push at the boundaries of traditional decorating wisdom.

Decorating tip Don't be afraid of combining different periods and styles of furniture but look for common elements – a colour, proportion or a material link – to ensure that they combine well.

CLEA Lawrence Durrell
FABER